CHASING MY DREAM

An African Immigrant Story in America

KOMI AFETSE

Ascendant
PRESS

www.ascendantpress.com

Book cover by Emily Edson Design

Library of Congress Cataloging-in-Publication Data in on file.

Paperback ISBN: 978 – 1 – 732 2973 – 0 – 2

Copyright Office Registration Number: TXu 2 – 085 – 719

Book Consulting Services by Ascendant Press
www.ascendant press.com

Table of Contents

Dedication

At the beginning, you have no choice of who your parents are, no choice of where you are born, and no choice in how you grow up. But as you mature, you become responsible for much of what happens to you.

Your outside world will not change unless you change your way of thinking. Once you do, everything around you will be the result of your mind's creation.

If you've ever wondered why you are here on this planet...

...if there's ever been a time in your life when nothing seemed to be going your way, but you kept going nevertheless...

...if you always feel like there is more to your life than your present conditions...

...if you are motivated to search for a better life and help others do the same...

...this book is for you.

Foreword

I remember vividly when Lieutenant Komi Afetse of the U.S. Army Reserve reached out to me on social media a couple years ago. He shared his appreciation for the work I do; and wanted to connect.

We got to know each other online—and six months later, we finally managed to meet in person when I was in Washington, D.C. for a conference. What was supposed to be a 45-minute dinner evolved into more than a two-hour conversation. I left feeling inspired by the story of a man who came to the United States with close to nothing—not even the English language—and fought through nearly impossible circumstances to achieve so many dreams. And he did it all with a positive attitude, a sense of gratitude, and a strong belief in the possibility for a better tomorrow.

Lt. Afetse came from a place where, even if one wanted to better himself, it would be close to impossible. Like me, he arrived in the United States with little more than the desire for an education and a wish to succeed. But that was enough to propel him toward his goals in a foreign land.

It wasn't easy. Lt. Afetse faced denied visa applications, immigration detention, and a string of challenges that included low-wage jobs and few resources. He confronted struggles that would make many say, "It wasn't meant to be." But Komi knew better. His heart and his faith told him that the land of opportunity had something for him too. He never wavered in his convictions. He absorbed inspiration and knowledge from everything and everyone around him. He seized every opportunity to move stealthily closer to his vision of becoming a leader in the United States Army.

This book is more than just a story of struggle and sacrifice. It is a testament to the power of a positive mindset and an optimistic worldview. Those positive mindsets can have a powerful impact on your ability to live your life, your way—despite the many roadblocks along the way.

This book is proof that immigrants, military members, and Americans as a whole have the power—and even a responsibility to themselves—to not only dream big, but to strive until those dreams are fulfilled.

It is a story of how your mindset affects everything in your life: from your outlook, to your relationships and your career opportunities. Positivity can be reflective—and Lt. Afetse's story is proof that the more you project, the more comes back to you.

Lt. Afetse teaches us that our beliefs about ourselves influence the choices we make. If we think we are nothing, we do nothing. If we think we are unworthy, everyone else will think so too. But if we believe we are creative, we will become more creative in our strategies to pursue success. And, Afetse says, if we believe we are worthy, we will take more opportunities, reach higher goals, and fight harder for happiness.

This book is for the people who want to accomplish more but feel held back by negative or unmotivated people. It is a book for those who want to break free to live a more inspired life. It is for those who want to learn how to surround themselves with positivity to expound on their own.

It is for military members to find their purpose, take advantage of the inspiring leaders at their disposal, and use the opportunity for service wisely in order to pave a path for success for the rest of their lives.

This book is for immigrants—or hopeful immigrants—to find the motivation to take advantage of the amazing opportunities in the United States. We want you to become the impactful, inspiring, successful self you have inside.

Lt. Afetse's remarks and insights are also for anyone who wants to learn the principles of perseverance, self-confidence, and crafting a winner's mindset. This book is for the people dreaming big but not doing big. It is for those craving a way to build their inner strength.

Lt. Afetse's story starts at the depths of desperate circumstances and ends in a triumph that continues today. I believe he will accomplish much more, continue to inspire, and make meaningful impact worldwide. His story is living proof that mindset makes or breaks success. And in these pages, you'll find the simple but powerful tools he's used to pull himself up. Take his advice for implementing those tools in your own life—right here, right now, and in whatever circumstance you find yourself when you pick up this book.

This book is for everyone who is ready to transcend negative circumstances, transform their thinking, and turn their dreams into their realities. I invite you to join me through these pages of Komi's inspiring story that begun over 5,000 miles away in Togo, West Africa and then ended in the realization of his American Dream.

Sincerely,

Marco Kpeglo LeRoc

Author, International Speaker, & Host of *Inside a Great Mind*

Preface

Why did I decide to write this book?

In February 2015, while I was deployed in Africa as a civil affairs specialist, I received my direct commission as a Second Lieutenant in the United States Army. A civil affairs specialist in the Army is primarily responsible for interacting with the civilian population anywhere the army is deployed. This person also serves as a bridge between military and civilian authorities during times of both peace and conflict. I went to Africa as a sergeant, but right before my deployment, I applied to become an officer. It was during this deployment that I was selected to commission as United States Army Officer.

Before taking the oath of office, I was asked to provide my background information to Major General Wayne Grigsby, the Commander of the Combined Joint Task Force in the Horn of Africa, who was going to administer the oath. After reading the biography I provided, the general asked me if he could share my story with his family. I was surprised and humbled that a two-star general in the United States Army—with all the life and professional experiences he had—wanted to share my story.

A few days after the ceremony, the Public Affairs Office of the Combined Joint Task Force in Horn of Africa asked me if I wanted to sit down for an interview. Would I extend my story with others as well? I met with SSgt Dean of the US Air Force and discussed how an immigrant from the small West African country of Togo had become an officer in the United States Army. My story was published on various military media outlets. And then for the next few months, I received many congratulatory handshakes, phone calls, and emails.

One of my teammates asked me, "Komi, why don't you share your story with everybody else in another platform like a book? Your experience could inspire people who are trying to do something similar—or even something totally different—to try little harder."

I wondered out loud who would want to read something about some random African immigrant living in the U.S. There are millions of immigrants just like me in this country. But he insisted that my story was unique, and that it could help someone else. After a long conversation with him, I promised to think about it.

As days and months went by, more and more emails of sincere congratulations and encouragement came in. One in particular caught my attention. It was from another service member who was originally from Africa but had moved to the U.S. a few years earlier. He joined the Army, too. It reads:

"Lieutenant Afetse,

I don't know you personally, but when I read your story, I felt like it was published just to encourage me to go relentlessly after my dream to become an Officer, too.

I am from South Africa, and I came to the U.S. a few years ago to find better opportunities for my family and myself. I had a master's degree from my home country, but still In my search, I encountered people who made me feel like it was impossible to become an officer, just because I was not born in the U.S.

I scratched my original plan and decided to go back to

school and just work in the civilian sector even though my true desire is to serve my new country. Reading your story was refreshing and motivating. So, I joined the army as an enlisted and now am in the process of becoming an officer. You truly encouraged me with your words even though we don't know each other. I stayed the course even though I was getting discouraged. Thank you for sharing."

After reading that email and thinking back at what my teammate said, I decided to record my experience here in the hopes that it would inspire someone else who might need a little encouragement. If an audiobook purchased in thrift store could revolutionize my life, then maybe my struggles, experiences, and victories could help others who are trying to do something with their lives. I wrote this book to let you know that you have a purpose in this life! I wrote this book to inspire you to dream big, work smart, achieve, and design your own life—regardless of where or how you were born.

Throughout my own journey, I have learned and applied many principles to overcome my challenges and keep my eyes on what I was trying to achieve. Principles such as belief, attitude, life philosophy, self-discipline, goal setting, time management, forgiveness, success, and many more were fundamental for me to be able to achieve every single goal I have set. I will share them with you in the hope that you can apply them on your own journey.

Of course, if nothing you've just read is news to you, I hope this book will remind you of what you already know. We all need that now and then.

PART I: **My Journey**

The Author's Letter

On the morning of March 24, 2014, I was sitting in my cubicle at U.S. Army Civil Affairs and Psychological Command headquarters office in Fort Bragg, North Carolina. Suddenly, something compelled me to glance at the calendar. As I looked, I realized that It was ten years ago since I arrived in my new country. I pulled out my pen and paper and allowed my thoughts to flow briefly capturing my first decade in the United States. Later that day, I posted the below to Facebook:

10 Years: A Letter from an African Immigrant (This will become the working title of my book)

(March 24, 2004 –March 24, 2014)

Ten years ago, on March 24, I landed in the United States of America to begin a new life.

I didn't have anything substantial. I didn't know many people. I didn't know where or how to begin. And I couldn't even spell my own name in English.

All I had was $165 in cash, three pairs of jeans, four t-shirts, and three pairs of shoes. I was full of hope, big dreams, and unwavering faith that I would make it in this land. My belief in the promises of America couldn't have been any higher.

I was armed with faith and determination to make

something out of myself. I couldn't have cared less about all the odds that were stacked against me. And there were plenty: language, education, culture, knowing the right people, having the right connections, etc. My motto was, "I will do what I have to do so I can do what I want to do."

Everything looked so different, so big, and so much better than my native Togo. I was overwhelmed. It was a great feeling, but at the same time it was paralyzing. I didn't know where to begin!

Ten years later, I am grateful for my life, my journey, and the opportunity to call this place my country. However, I would be lying if I told you that it was easy to get where I am today. I would be lying if I said coming to America as a student was easy. I would be lying if I said going through the immigration process was fun. I would be lying if I said working two to three minimum wage jobs at the same time was entertaining. I would be lying if I said working six to seven days a week for many years was enjoyable. I would be lying if I said being a taxi driver, a nightclub bathroom attendant, a bellman, a doorman, or a concierge was always satisfying. I would be lying if I said being an adult learning a new language from ABC to 123 and then pursuing a college degree was an easy task. I would be lying if I told you that working on Thanksgiving, Christmas, and every other holiday was pleasant.

In short, I would be lying if I said I didn't have to work very hard and sacrifice a lot. But you know what? I didn't care. I was just happy that I had those jobs, and I was working on moving ahead. I kept my eyes on my aspirations, and it paid off.

So, let me tell you about what I learned and, most importantly, who I have become along this incredible, ten-year journey. Hard work, opportunity, perseverance, and hope for a better future are still alive in this country. If you know what you really want, and you are determined to get it, it is all possible here.

I learned to be patient, humble, and grateful for everything no matter what the situation looked like. I learned that I can achieve whatever dreams I can conceive in my mind and believe in my heart. I learned that hanging out with people who are going nowhere with their lives is a sure way to stall mine.

I learned that goals are the most powerful prayers I can address to God. I learned that I was not who I thought I was, but I was what was in my mind. I learned that I must define and create my own happiness. I learned that sometimes I might not know exactly how things occur, but it is not my job to figure all that out. All I need is faith in my God!

And finally, I learned that I am becoming what I think about all day long.

Otherwise, how can I explain where I am today? For example, show me a first-generation immigrant to France, Germany, England, China, Russia, or elsewhere serving as a military officer in less than ten years after immigrating to that country. I am not 100 percent sure they do not exist, but they must be rare. Here in the United States so many of us have achieved that dream. I could go on with many examples, but there's no need.

America provided me with the same rights, protection, and privileges as they provide to those who are born here. And America provided me with the opportunity to be who I have always wanted to be. This country allowed me to earn an advanced college education through the Army. I've also earned a beautiful place I call home, a loving family, a promising career, my dream house, all the material things I can think of, and the ability to become a better person so I can give myself to others. Above all, it's given me the chance to realize every single desire of my heart.

My journey from March 24, 2004 to today convinced me more than ever that I am headed in the right direction. I am confident that my life will get better and better if I stay the course and never give up on my dreams. I am not a fortune-teller, nor am I God. I don't know what is in my future, but I am convinced it can only get better. I am on my way to my destiny. Since nothing in this world is perfect, my life in America is still a work in progress. It is a continuous journey of trials, tribulations, setbacks, delays, failures, and denials.

However, there are also many joyful moments of triumph, success over defeats and adversities, and happy memories that will last for a lifetime.

My story isn't different from a lot of immigrants who travelled the same path in search of a better life in America. However, I want to share mine in to encourage those who might be struggling to keep up with a new life—whether they've moved to a new country or they're going through changes at home.

I didn't get where I am overnight. It took time, courage, failures, and perseverance. Ten years ago I came here with only hope, faith, determination, a couple bucks in my pocket, and unwavering belief in the promises of this nation. I was in the same place as so many others are today.

When I look back at those trials, I am grateful for every single one. So, don't let anybody tell you that you are just an immigrant, you are not good enough, or you can't make it because of your accent. Keep your dream alive; and go for it! The lessons can be applied anywhere on this planet, but I learned them in this magical place called the United States of America.

Sincerely,

Komi

CHAPTER 1
My Belief

Believe it can be done. When you believe something can be done, really believe, your mind will find the ways to do it. Believing a solution paves the way to solution. —David J. Schwartz

Is there a force out there—a God, an essence, or an unnamed power—that is can bring anything you really desire into your life? Or is life just a result of random events?

Personally, I believe there is a God—though you can call it a higher power, the Universe or anything you prefer.

I was born with a high degree of curiosity. In my youth I struggled a lot with big questions about human conditions on earth: life, death, joy, health, purpose, fame, success, and failure. Why do some people succeed, and others fail? Why are some constantly sick, and others enjoy healthy lives? How can two people born from the same parents follow such drastically different paths? Why are some considered very lucky while others are so unlucky?

These questions tormented me, and I wanted to know the answers so badly that I was drawn to anything mystical in nature that could provide me with insights. Early on, I started reading books related to the spiritual realm: voodoo, magic, metaphysics, religion, and anything else I thought could give me an explanation.

Some books were strange, some made sense, and others were nonsensical. However, I noticed a common trait that linked all these books. Whether they were about Hinduism, Islam, Christianity, voodoo, metaphysics, or magic, they all emphasized belief as the key that would bring their followers what they wanted in their lives.

There is a popular notion that our destiny is already pre-determined and nothing can be done about it, but I strongly believe that we can change our destinies. If you realize who you are and what you have available to you, you can control the way your life turns out.

Let me ask you this question: if you buy a new gadget or appliance, and you take it home without any instructions, will you be able to use it efficiently? Of course not! You might get some very basic usage out of it, but without the instruction manual, you'll have very little success.

Unfortunately, we humans do not come with instruction manuals. We must be taught most of the things we know. As adults we are often left to figure things out as we go. This doesn't help us get very far ahead. Unless we truly learn the rules for success, we often live lives of quiet desperation.

We are born into a universe that is governed by many sets of rules, and not knowing these guidelines will not excuse you from the consequences of violating them. On the other hand, knowing and applying them will make a great difference in your future.

According to Genevieve-Gold Flight, there are twelve laws of the universe:

1. The Law of Divine Oneness: Everything is connected to everything else. Every thought, word, action and belief affect others and the universe around us, irrespective of whether the people are near or far away—in other words, beyond time and space.

2. The Law of Vibration: Everything in the universe vibrates, moves, and travels in circular patterns. The same principle of vibration in the physical world applies to our feelings, desires, thoughts, dreams, and will. Each sound, thought, or thing has its own unique vibrational frequency.

3. The Law of Perpetual Transmutation of Energy: We all have power within us to change any condition in our lives that we are not happy with. Higher-energy vibrations will definitely consume and transform lower ones. Therefore, we can change the energies in our lives by understanding the universal laws and applying the principles. We can make a positive change in our lives.

4. The Law of Polarity: Everything is on a continuum, and everything has an opposite. There has to be darkness, so we might appreciate light. There is solid and liquid, and we can see and feel the differences. We have the ability to suppress and transform undesirable thoughts by focusing on the opposite thoughts, thereby bringing about the desired positive changes. This could also be likened to the law of mental vibration.

5. The Law of Rhythm: Everything vibrates and moves to a certain rhythm. This rhythm establishes cycles, seasons, patterns, and stages of development. Each cycle is a reflection of the regularity of God's universe. To master each rhythm, you must rise above any negative part of the cycle.

6. The Law of Gender: Everything has both its masculine (yang) and feminine (yin) principles, and these are the basis for all creation. As spiritual beings, we must ensure that there

is a balance between the masculine and feminine energies within us in order to become true co-creators with God.

7. The Law of Action: We must engage in actions that support our words, feelings, visions, thoughts, dreams, and emotions. These actions will manifest various results that are dependent on our specifically chosen words, thoughts, dreams, and emotions.

8. The Law of Correspondence: We are in the driver's seat of our own lives. Our outer world is a direct reflection of our inner world; therefore, we need to accept responsibility for our own lives.

9. The Law of Attraction: We create the events, people and things that come into our lives. All our thoughts, words, feelings, and actions give out energies that attract like-energies. Positive energies will always attract positive energies, while negative energies will always attract negative energies. It doesn't matter whether you want the negative or not. What you focus on is what you attract into your life.

10. The Law of Compensation: The various forms of compensation we receive in life are the visible effects of our direct and indirect actions carried out throughout our lives.

11. The Law of Relativity: We will all encounter a series of situations or problems designed to strengthen the "inner light" within us. This law also teaches us to compare our situations to other people's problems and put everything into its right perspective. No matter how badly we perceive our situations to be, there is always someone who is in a more difficult or worse situation. Everything is relative.

12. The Law of Cause and Effect: Nothing happens by chance or outside the universal laws. This means that we must take responsibility for everything that happens in our lives. Every action has an equal reaction or consequence, and we reap what we sow. You cannot plant a hibiscus and expect to grow a rose. In other words, every thought, action, and word is full of energy.

The most powerful of all these laws, in my personal opinion, is the Law of Cause and Effect. Your belief and actions are the causes, and the details of your life are the effects. It is that simple. The quicker you understand this law, the better off you will be for the rest of your life. Work with it, and you will be surprised by the results.

This book does not adhere to any specific religion. Whether you are Christian, Muslim, atheist, or a follower of any other of the hundreds or thousands of religions out there, the principles and reflections in this book are meant to help you achieve the life you desire.

However, just like the mystical and religious books I read when I was young, this book focuses on belief. The belief I am referring to is that deep-down feeling you have about yourself and the life you want to live. Your belief about yourself is the engine that will take you places. The belief I am alluding to is nothing mystical; however, it is unknown to many. This belief is powerful, and when you discover this force and put it to proper use, your life can go in any direction you want it to.

We all have many beliefs about our overall abilities, the reasons for our achievements or failures, and our relationship to the external world. These self-beliefs influence the goals we set, the tasks we embrace, the strategies we use, and what we will ultimately accomplish with our lives. I would like to start by relating how I came to use this force to jump-start my life into the direction I wanted.

My Early Years

I was born and raised in the West African country of Togo. I lived in a traditional African family: father, mother, many brothers, sisters, cousins, nieces, nephews, uncles, aunts, grandparents and so on.

Togo is bordered by Ghana to the west, Benin to the east, and Burkina Faso to the north. It extends south to the Gulf of Guinea, where its capital, Lomé, is located. Slightly smaller than West Virginia, Togo covers 57,000 square kilometers (22,008 square miles), making it one of the smallest countries in Africa, with a population of approximately 7.6 million people.

My dad worked for a French company for well over thirty years while my mother was a homemaker. My mother was the second of my father's four wives, and I was the eleventh of his eighteen children. So, I grew up in a very large family with many brothers, sisters, cousins, uncles, and other relatives. My father took care of all of us financially.

This large family was not unusual in the Togolese culture. If there was one person who had a decent job and stable income, it was that person's moral responsibility to take care of the other, less fortunate members of the family. In my family, my dad was that person.

Nothing about my childhood foreshadowed who and where I am today. My "destiny," according to my parents' expectations, was to follow the traditional path of finishing school, getting a job, getting married, and raising a family in Togo.

As far as religion, I grew up a Protestant because my parents were Protestants. In fact, my grandfather was the first Christian in my family. He was baptized by German missionaries working in Togo in the early 1900s. I went to church most Sundays, and I was taught to pray to God and ask for forgiveness for my sins to avoid going to hell. I followed these church rituals without any real understanding.

Whenever something couldn't be explained, we were told that only God had the answer. For example, when I asked why one of my sisters was constantly sick, my parents always replied that only God knew the answer.

Most of the church teachings were focused on life after death. Paradise and hell dominated every conversation, in or out of church. However, no one ever taught me about how life works, or what I needed to do to get ahead. As far as I knew, praying was all about keeping God happy to avoid punishment by some incurable disease or death and eternal condemnation to hell. There were no practical teachings about how to live on this earth, and no one explained to me that I could forge my own destiny by controlling my thoughts and my focus.

As I mentioned earlier, I was very curious about life and why things happened the way they did. When I was twelve years old, my best friend brought one of his dad's books to school: The Game of Life and How to Play It by Florence Scovel Shinn. He showed it to me during our lunch break, and we read the summary in the back of the book.

At that age, I didn't know anything about the conscious and the subconscious mind, and neither of us could completely understand what this book was really about. However, a portion of the summary talked about how you can bring anything into your life if you know how to use your subconscious. This part stayed with me for a long time. Even though I was twelve years old, I had the feeling that there was a much better life somewhere beyond my Togolese "destiny." Even then, I recall looking at kids with fancy toys and games and wondering why I couldn't be one of these kids. Why couldn't things be better for me?

So, the title of this book, The Game of Life and How to Play It, intrigued me; and I wanted to know more. But since I didn't have time to read the book and try to understand more, I was operating with very little information. My friend had to return the book that same day because his father had forbidden him to read it since it was not for children.

I wish I could understand why I came in contact with this book so long before I would be able to read it and take advantage of its insights. Nevertheless, the brief encounter and the little understanding I was able to glean from the summary accidently set me on my life's journey. I never stopped believing that I was destined for something bigger, that I was here on this earth for a purpose, and that it was up to me to discover that purpose.

Today, I believe I have found my life's purpose, which is to make something out of my life and then help others do the same.

As the years went by, that little voice inside me only grew louder. It kept telling me to keep looking for that better life, not stopping until I discovered it. At times I got completely lost because I would copy people around me and try to be like everybody else. However, that little voice always brought me back on track.

If you are reading this book, I'm sure you know that you and I have this in common. You know deep inside that you are destined for an uncommon life, yet the noise and distractions of others often pull you off track.

Let me encourage you not to tune out your inner voice. Pick yourself up instead. Find your way back to your own path. My belief led me to share my story with you today, and my question to you is where will your belief take you? There is something unique and special programmed inside you, and only you can manifest it into this world. Are you going to let it die?

When I look back at my life and see what some of my childhood friends have become compared to where I am, I am very humbled, grateful, and amazed at how far my journey has taken me. Why did our lives take such very different paths? I cannot answer this with

100 percent certainty, but I suspect the difference lies in what we believe ourselves to be. So, I am encouraging you to analyze your own beliefs and see where they stand. This fundamental feeling about yourself and your abilities is what separates you from the rest of the human race.

This desire for a better life never left me, and it helped me immeasurably along my journey. Ultimately, how you see yourself is the best indicator of who you will become. Have you thought about how you see yourself? How do you feel about your own abilities? Do this personal assessment today. It could be the beginning of a total transformation.

CHAPTER 2
Getting my American Visa

Nobody is plotting to get inside Poland. Nobody is saying only if I can go to China. Everybody wants to come here! Why? Because this is where everything you need to be successful is: the books, the libraries, the opportunities, and, most importantly, the freedom to be your own person! — Jim Rohn

The American Dream tells you that, through hard work and determination, you can achieve success. It has its roots in the Declaration of Independence: "all men are created equal" with the right to "Life, liberty, and the pursuit of happiness." The Dream tells you that in America, people of any class, religion, or race can "make it" without the barriers to upward social mobility. That's why so many people came to America, and continue to do so, in hopes of a better life, a level playing field, and the chance to start over. — Emma Murphy

Deciding to leave your native country is not always easy. We all have a special attachment to our places of birth, the homes where we grew up, the people, the culture, and the places we grew accustomed to. But there could be any number of motivations to leave: political, economic, social, or religious, to name just a few.

I left my home country for the simple fact that I wanted a better education, better opportunities in life, and a higher chance to become who I knew I could be.

As I reflect on my childhood, I don't see how I could have made it in my native country of Togo. The political system was not a democratic one, and everything was tied to "who you know." For example, getting a decent job after studies required a "connection" inside the administration or company you wanted to work for. The fabric of the political, economic, and social systems was tangled. Almost everything was quid pro quo.

I came from a very modest family, and I just knew that I wasn't going to amount to much in that kind of setting. It would have been very easy to give up and resign myself to a life of mediocrity. How I managed to get out of there and make it to where I am today is still a mystery to me. We cannot always comprehend how things happen, and that is why faith—in yourself and in any higher entity you believe in—is crucial.

A Visa to the U.S.

For someone from Togo, a visa for United States of America is equivalent to a ticket to Paradise for Christians seeking the afterlife. If you don't believe me, conduct your own little survey next time you encounter an immigrant from Togo. Just ask this simple question: How difficult was the process to come to the United States?

Let me give you some perspective. Getting a visa to go to most European countries required being rich or having "connections" that could help you do so. It was an open secret that most European visas were "for sale" to the highest bidders. However, to obtain an American visa, connections and bribery were not going to help. This visa could only be obtained by legal means. The United States Embassy gave people like me hope that I could be given a chance once I met the requirements. All I needed to do was follow the process step by step.

In Togo, whenever we heard someone was going to America, the sentiment was that that person was "saved" from the lack of opportunity, grimy future, and limited options that characterized living in Togo. I have no ill will toward my home country, but those were the conditions of growing up there.

On the other hand, the name "America" has such powerful resonance throughout the entire world, for better or worse, and my native Togo wasn't immune to its influence. Thanks to Hollywood movies and firsthand accounts from people who visited the U.S., America was and still is considered heaven on earth—a place where everything is possible.

Hollywood has presented the United States so well to the outsiders. Coming here can be equated to getting a blank check in life. You can write in any amount you so desire and take it to the bank. American-made movies such as Forrest Gump, and countless pop songs by hundreds of artists painted a truly optimistic view of American society. The only thing is, unlike a movie, that success takes more than ninety minutes to materialize.

I first heard about this great land in my history and geography class. Part of our school's ninth-grade curriculum required the study of all continents. We learned about all of them, but America was the only one that stuck—particularly my teacher's special emphasis on the United States.

My teacher was in love with this country. Even though he never had a chance to visit, he had read everything about America. And he knew how to communicate his passion to his students. My instructor talked about this land as the "promised land," emphasizing the great achievements people from this part of the world.

As he taught about the two world wars, he argued that without the United States' involvement, the world as we know it might not even exist. He mentioned that America helped saved Europe during both wars, and later helped rebuild the European continent.

He loved referring to America as the "melting pot"—the place where multiple cultures from around the world lived in harmony. He talked about how anybody from anywhere in the world could enter this land without a penny in their pocket and go on to make a fortune, transforming their lives for the better. In short, my teacher awakened in me the obsession with coming to this country.

From ninth grade on, I became determined to experience this "magical" place for myself. Because we all spoke French, most of my classmates dreamed of going to France, where jobs were available. One could earn higher incomes—even in the entry-level jobs— than they could in Togo.

However, when I learned about the United States of America, I all but forgot about France. All I talked about was the fact that I was going to see this "promised land." Whenever my friends asked me how I was going to achieve this dream, knowing how complex it is to leave Togo, I told them I would find a way. At the time, I knew nothing about how this would occur.

But during my first year of college, just one year after graduating from high school, I applied for a student visa.

I cannot describe my excitement leading up to my first interview. All I could think about—all I had dreamed about—was America. This was my chance to study, work, and achieve my goals.

Back then, I knew of four ways to get the American visa: diversity lottery visa, business visa, tourism visa, and students' visa.

The Diversity Immigrant Visa Program (DV) is a U.S. Government

Program administered by the Department of State. It is designed to make fifty thousand immigrant visas available annually to individuals who are from countries with low rates of immigration to the United States. Togo is part of this program, and participation was simple. All a candidate had to do was fill out one page of information with a passport photo attached. About ten months later, a random drawing would determine which candidates would be selected. Luck is obviously a major factor, but I wasn't lucky. I entered my name every year since 1998, but I was never selected.

Business and tourism, as you can guess by their names, were for business people and tourists. So, the only visa I qualified to apply for was the student visa. I applied. The next step was the official interview at the United States embassy.

My First Visa Interview

I was too excited to sleep the night before my first interview on December 31, 2001. By three o'clock in the morning I was ready. I left the house and took my place in line outside the U.S. Embassy compound before five o'clock. Even though the embassy doesn't open until seven in the morning, by the time I got there, there was already a very long line. I cannot tell you how many people waited that day, but the line reminded me of Apple customers in line for a new gadget release.

The excitement turned quickly into nerves as the embassy doors opened and the line started moving. I walked through the doors. The air conditioning sent a cold chill into my bones. I had put all my hopes into getting this visa. I wanted to leave a country where success depended on what your last name was, who you knew, and who knew you.

I couldn't conceive of a future in Togo, and I didn't know what I would do if the interview didn't go well. I really don't want to generalize my personal experience—not every Togo citizen feels the way I felt. However, most of my generation and the generation before were highly motivated to leave Togo. We wanted to forge a new future elsewhere. The more I thought about it, the more anxious I became. Suddenly, answers to basic questions were escaping my mind.

Everybody has anxiety when preparing for a job interview, first date, or any situation where a few minutes of face-to-face time will determine some big piece of your future. I am sure you can recall a time when you felt like everything hung in the balance of a single moment. If you multiply that feeling by one hundred, maybe you can imagine how I was feeling that day.

If you are born in United States of America, you can probably never fully understand the level of anxiety about interviewing to get an America visa. By nine o'clock my interview was over, and I had received devastating news: I was denied the visa.

So many feelings crashed down upon me. I felt that I lost my soul, that my life was over, and that there was nothing left to do except wait until death took me.

Depending on how you grew up, this setback might seem insignificant, but that visa was my ticket to a better life. When I left the embassy after my interview, I went to a friend's house and slept. It was New Year's Eve, and I had no desire to go out and celebrate. Instead, I went through the stages of disappointment, sadness, and more sadness. I was completely lost. I didn't know what to do, and it took me four months to get over that single defeat.

Later, I pulled my thoughts together enough to consider the consular officer's reason for denying me the visa that day. The interview itself was not a difficult exchange. It was just basic questions about who you are, your educational background, and your study plan. On the other side, the consular officer determined a candidate's eligibility based on some criteria that I was not familiar with. My fate was in the hand of this person who interviewed me.

It is funny how we choose to hear only what we want to hear in a given situation. We just tune out everything else, even if it's for our own good. I tuned out after that interview, and I never understood why my first attempts were denied beyond the generic explanation that I did not meet the requirements. There could have been a specific reason or no reason at all.

But despite the rejection and the searing disappointment, I was eligible to come back in six months. My application could be reexamined.

I firmly decided that I would go back and apply again, since I knew deep inside me that my destiny was to become a citizen of the United States of America.

I applied for the same visa four years in a row, from 2001 to 2004. Finally, on March 12, 2004, I was granted the visa to study in America.

Tony Robbins said, "I've come to believe that all my past failures and frustrations were actually laying the foundation for the understandings that have created the new level of living I now enjoy."

I believe if you truly want something—whether it's a specific field of study or a visa or anything else—and you get rejected, you should keep trying until you earn your place. Going through this process for four years, I was resolved to keep trying. This was my first big victory in applying the principle of perseverance.

CHAPTER 3
My First Day in America

I departed Togo on Tuesday, March 23, 2004, around 10:00 p.m. local time and arrived in the United States on Wednesday, March 24, 2004, at Cincinnati/Northern Kentucky International Airport around 3:00 p.m. EST. As I presented myself at the immigration officer for entry formalities, the officer carefully examined my passport and attached documents. After a few questions, he asked me to step aside. Minutes went by. Then a female officer approached and asked me to follow her into a small room not too far down the hallway.

The next three hours would be unforgettable. My luggage was searched, and then I was interrogated, patted down, and handcuffed. Here is a more detailed account of my first day in my beloved America as I wrote in my personal journal later.

Date: March 24th, 2004
Time: 8:45 p.m., Eastern Time
Location: Cincinnati / Northern Kentucky International Airport
Parties involved: Komi M. Afetse vs U.S. Immigration and Customs Enforcement

After an intensive, three-hour interrogation session (during which I replied "yes" to almost everything the immigration officer was asking me, due to my limited English comprehension), I was placed in a holding cell at the airport by Immigration and Customs authorities. My crime: I arrived late to my university, and I had not informed the school authorities that I would be doing so.

I was late because after my visa was issued, there was no flight available that would allow me to arrive on time for class. My visa was issued on March 12, 2004, and classes were scheduled to begin on March 15. But the earliest flight available was on March 23. I booked that flight, intending to arrive at the university as soon as possible. I should have contacted the school to inform them.

The immigration officer called the school, which told him that they were not expecting me. It wasn't unusual for international students to come late and begin class the very next semester. But late arrival required proper documentation. They had taken my absence on the first day of class as a sign that I would not be coming at all.

In hindsight, this was clearly a simple protocol fumble. Unfortunately for me, it meant I was denied entry onto U.S. soil. I was upset. But I reminded myself that it had only been only three years since September 11, 2001; and the terrorists were students here in America too.

Eight hours after arriving in America, I was still sitting in that very small room at the airport, waiting for somebody to determine my fate. All I could think was, why is this happening to me? I told you, didn't I?

Since the moment I stepped off the plane in Cincinnati, my life in my new home has been a wild roller coaster ride.

Jail Details

My first night in the United States of America was spent on the floor inside a county jail in Cincinnati, Ohio. The first photograph taken of me in the United States was a mug shot. In fact, if you

Google my name, I believe you can still see this picture online. I was devastated. But in the middle of all this turmoil, I just paid attention to the small voice that was still inside me. It was telling me not to lose hope, because somehow everything would be fine.

The beautiful thing about this country that I love so dearly and serve with pride is that the laws are here to protect its people. Though it would take me years to understand, I know now that my unfortunate incarceration was not personal. The officer who arrested me was doing his job.

For almost four months after my arrival, I was in immigration custody. During this time two things happened to me. First, I became more determined to make something out of my life. Second, I saw firsthand what happened in immigration custody.

America is truly a magnet for people from all over the world. Immigration custody is exclusively for foreign-born individuals who have allegedly violated immigration laws, either while living in or coming to the United States. These violations ranged from overstaying visas to arriving illegally. The violations can also be minor issues at immigration checkpoints to permanent residents who had lost their status due to a crime or alleged crime.

I met many people from all over the world: Africa, South America, Asia, Europe, the Middle East, and more. Some were fighting deportation, some were waiting to be released, and others were counting the days until they would appear before immigration judges to plead their cases.

For four months I lived in a controlled environment where I had to wake up at a certain time for "headcount". I ate breakfast, lunch, and dinner when they were served. Going "outside" in the yard was a privilege I had to earn, and I did not get to choose which TV station to watch. If you have never watched any prison documentary, I would recommend one called Lockup. It will show you exactly how I lived for almost 120 days.

Some of the people I met and talked to during my detention were very optimistic. Some were simply confused, and still others had given up hope for making it in America. I found that our moods were contagious. I could rapidly become depressed or confused depending on who I spent time with. So, I learned quickly who to talk to and who to avoid.

A typical day during began with headcount at 5:30 a.m. followed by breakfast from 6:00 to 7:30 a.m. From 8:00 to 10:30 a.m. was my personal time to either read a book I had borrowed from a guy named Patrick or go to a morning prayer group that four other inmates and I had formed. The group members were Patrick from Gabon, Oboh from Nigeria, Douglas from Jamaica, and Abel from Ethiopia. We prayed mostly about our situations, and we cried out to God to strengthen us until he could free us.

Among my jail friends, I spoke to Patrick the most, for the simple reason that he was from Gabon, a French-speaking country. Patrick had lived in America for ten years. He had a permanent residency card, and he was married with two children. He told me that he was in immigration detention because of domestic violence charges. He claimed his innocence and told me that the real problem was his wife's marital infidelity, which he had discovered a couple years earlier. He confronted her about it, which led to their dispute. The police got involved, and he was prosecuted in the criminal court and convicted of assault and other charges. Any permanent resident of the United States of America found guilty of certain crimes, including assault, must face immigration judges to defend their continued residence.

Oboh was an engineering student from Nigeria who got into some troubles, though he never told anyone exactly what his case was. Douglas, from Jamaica, said he was being deported for a crime he committed fifteen years earlier. Abel, from Ethiopia, had been arrested at the airport for failing to declare something in his luggage. I met many more people with various stories but spent most of my time with those four.

Lunch was served from 11:00 a.m. to 12:30 p.m. During the afternoon, one hour was reserved for time in the yard or in my bed, depending on the day. Dinner was from 4:30 to 5:30 p.m. Showers were open between 6:00 and 7:00 p.m. By 9:00 p.m. I had to stand by my bed like everyone else for another headcount. Lights were out by 10:00 p.m.

On the days that inmates went to court, they woke up around 3:00 a.m. and usually did not return until 5:00 p.m. As soon as they returned, everyone else was eager to hear about the outcome.

It was during this time I realized that an individual can challenge the U.S. government in court and win. This was a surprise. Nothing like this could happen in Togo. Anyone who has any issue with the government there is considered guilty, simple as that. Even if you go to court, it's probably for show.

Appearance Before the Judge

My first appearance before the immigration judge was via television screen, with the assistance of a French interpreter. After I stated my full name, the judge read all the charges against me and asked me if I had a lawyer. I did not. I was not sure what the judge told the prosecutor, but he decided to set another date to give me time to find a lawyer.

As this process continued, it was clear to me that this federal judge had the power to determine whether I could stay in the U.S. or be sent back to Togo. Some of the inmates with whom I shared the details of my case told me that I could be stuck in detention for two or more years waiting for the process to conclude. They advised me to sign voluntary departure papers so I could be returned quickly to Togo.

By now you know how much I wanted to come here and create my future, so you can imagine my response to that suggestion. I didn't want to go back. Even though I was not too familiar with the American justice system at the time, I was confident that my case was just a complete misunderstanding, and that I would be released. Still, the ones who had given up fighting thought I was crazy not to request a voluntary trip back to Togo.

I didn't know at that time how things would turn out for me, but I was not ready for my dream to collapse. I was willing to fight for my future. I gladly accepted temporary detention until I pled my case to the judge. Then I would accept whatever outcome resulted.

The second time I went before the judge, I had hired a Chicago lawyer. I got the attorney's number from another inmate. My lawyer requested another court date so he had more time to prepare my defense. On my third and fourth court appearances, the judge saw what I saw: a clear misunderstanding. The charges were dismissed, and the judge signed off my conditional release. The case was resolved completely years later; and I was officially allowed to stay.

On August 19, 2004, the handcuffs were removed. I was released from immigration custody in Chicago, Illinois. As I walked outside, I knelt down, and kissed the ground. The officer who escorted me out looked at me a little strangely, but I didn't care. I knew he couldn't understand or appreciate my happiness and satisfaction.

During this detention, I kept the possibilities ahead in mind, and my faith, belief, and my inner strength grew to unimaginable heights. I became confident in my ability to forge my own destiny.

The detention experience forced me to rely on a strength I could not see. When properly used, that force could help me achieve anything I wanted. This experience led me to believe that there is no such thing as coincidence. Everything that happens is a lesson. Every setback can lead to great opportunities.

In life, it is up to you to open your eyes and see what you can make out of every situation—no matter how bad it seems in the moment. Had I given into the suggestion of signing a voluntary departure and returning to Togo just because I didn't want to wait in detention or fight for what I believed was right, I don't think I would be sharing these lines with you today. I believed deeply that coming to America was my destiny, regardless of what anybody said or what situation I found myself in that very first day.

CHAPTER 4
My First Year

On August 19, 2004, couple hours after my release from immigration custody in Chicago, I boarded a Greyhound bus headed to Silver Spring, Maryland. Some family friends had arranged my trip, buying my ticket in advance. They made a plan for me to get to the bus stop in Chicago. For nineteen hours I sat on that bus, riding across the Midwest to my destination.

I sat by the window, which allowed me to see the beauty of this land for the first time. We traveled through beautiful sections of Illinois, Indiana, Ohio, and Pennsylvania to Maryland. Anytime we approached a different city, the driver announced the upcoming stop. I did not understand everything, so I always looked outside the window to see if I could see any sign to let me know where we were. Along the away travelers got on and off. I lost track of time as I fell in and out of sleep.

During this long ride, I had time again to contemplate my life, and I was more grateful than ever to be free to pursue my destiny in my new home country.

I arrived in Silver Spring, Maryland on August 20, 2004, around 3:30 p.m. local time. I was welcomed by a family friend who helped me and carried my luggage to the taxi. We went home. And for the first time in four months, I had a home-cooked meal. I was so grateful not to be eating jail food. On my first night in detention, I had been given a tray of mashed potatoes, some vegetable, chicken, and a fruit cup for dinner. In Togo, the main dish was always rice, corn, or yam based. I had never eaten American food before I arrived in the jail. Eventually I got used to American dishes, but they were nothing compared to that first home-cooked meal in Silver Spring.

After dinner I took a shower and went straight to bed. I was exhausted. Really, bed was a sofa in the living room, because it was one-bedroom apartment that housed four adults and one child. I was the fifth adult. It was so kind and generous of them to accommodate me. I stayed there for the next six weeks until another family friend agreed to take me in. As a fresh immigrant, there was little I could say or do on my own. I was at the mercy of anyone who wanted to help me.

My next residence was a two-bedroom condominium. The owner, his wife, and their two sons stayed in the master bedroom. I shared the second room with another person. After I settled in, the big question arose: where do I start? It became clear to me that I was going to have to work extra hard to achieve even very basic things. I was an adult who did not speak English and who had not been educated in America. How could I do anything in a country where I couldn't understand anyone? It became clear that if I was going to amount to anything, I had to learn to speak English well—and quickly.

Values and Culture

A while ago a co-worker brought to my attention an article he read about the high probability of immigrants achieving a lot more in various areas of their lives. They tend to do so in education, income level, and so on compared to people born here in America. He asked me my thoughts on this. I told him that I do not have the data nor the author's expertise. But here is what I know from my own experience and the experiences of countless immigrants I met.

Every immigrant who steps foot in America came from a place with limited resources or was missing something in their lives. They see something lacking before leaving their home countries. They come to the United States with a burning desire to either rebuild the life they lost or create a new and better one. This place called America is unique. Desires mixed with certain values and views in life are what I personally think make a lot of difference.

Growing up in Togo, it is true that the political system is considered muddled. The country lacked basic structure to provide adequate services to its population. There are many other deficiencies that made it difficult for the average person in Togo to get ahead.

However, there is something fundamentally unique about the education and values I received from my parents that prepared me to do well in the United States of America. I think good, solid parental training is shared among many Africans, at least people from Togo. My parents taught me many important values. I would like to detail those values in this book, but I think I will reserve some of that for later. However, one value that I believe carried me the most through my life so far-- and I can trace its root back to my childhood--is resilience.

What do I mean? The simplest definition of resilience I came across is the capacity to recover quickly from difficulties. It is also the process of adjusting well to adversity by drawing on personal and social resources. Being resilient was embedded in my soul at a very early age. I was taught to be grateful and not complain about anything.

I remembered whenever I was whining to my mother about wearing the same clothes or shoes for a week or two, she will look me in the eyes. With her steady glaze she would ask if I preferred giving my clothing to the neighbor kids who didn't even have that. Then she will use the opportunity to lecture me and my siblings about how we should be grateful and not complain.

I was also taught to be respectful and polite to everybody regardless of their age or social status. In my culture I cannot call someone older than me by their first name. Instead, I use respectful generic titles such as uncle, auntie, and others that I couldn't find translation for.

Today, every time anyone asks me about finding the strength and courage to work through many of my challenges, I simply smile and reply: "I have seen worse".

Most African children see a great amount of tragedy by the time they turn 10. The same situations would break down their peers born at the same time in America or any other developed country, for this matter.

Many African cultures focus on dealing and copping effectively with whatever is going on. We are taught to remain hopeful. In Togo there is popular word in my native language. The Ewe word is: "elava-gnon", meaning "it will get better".

There is even a popular fable. I do not know where it originated but it illustrates the resilience of most Africans you will meet. It contains our philosophy of life. It goes like this: God called for a meeting where all seven continents sent a representative to give Him an update on life in their respective continents and what He can do to help each them.

The European representative walked up first and said: "God, everything is going well for us. We have achieved the highest living standards on earth, and we are successful in genetically modifying our food resulting in feeding everybody. So, we are in good shape. The only thing we ask is to grant us the power to reduce the winter or summer seasons as we see them fit." With a smile, God replied: "I will see what I can do."

An Asia representative reported next, and said "God, thank you for the opportunity you have given us the last 50 years to turn life around in our continent. We have reduced the poverty level, doubled our literacy rate, and increased food production. We have also achieved some level of success in medicine to take care of our people. All we are asking for is to keep this opportunity going for the next 100 years". With a smile, God replied: "I will see what I can do."

The North America representative asked God: "We are actively looking for life on other planets such as Mars, and we want to know if there are any and what can you do to help. We have conquered life here on earth already." With a smile, God replied: "I will see what I can do."

The South America representative asked God about eliminating earthquakes completely. God replied: "I will see what I can do" with a smile.

An Antarctica representative commented on his continent's cold weather. The Australia representative asked God to help eliminate all the dangerous wild animals roaming around. To both requests God smiled and replied: "I will see what I can do."

Finally came the African representative. As he approached God's throne, the smile on God's face disappeared. Tears started to flow in God's eyes and He began to cry inconsolably. The previously joyful atmosphere turned to deep sadness. Puzzled by the quick turn of the events, the African representative was confused and began consoling God. He murmured "God why are you crying? Did I do anything to upset you? Please don't cry!" God said, "I am aware of Africa and its problems."

The African representative continued to speak. "On behalf on my continent all we want is very simple: we want all wars to stop. We want to get rid of famines and have a chance to just live in peace. Can you help with that?" To this God, still crying, replied: "I know what your continent has been going through, and I will do my best to help you during the next 300 years".

Since resilience and hope are the strong suits of Africans in general, without any hesitation or questions, or asking for God to do this sooner, the African representative nodded and departed.

As a kid, I would go out and play for hours with friends. We never cared about fancy toys, or anything that involved spending a lot of money to enjoy ourselves. We made our own toys out of wood or anything we could find. It was fun.

In my childhood community, everyone will watch and care for everyone else. Anyone could supervise neighborhood kids and punish them if necessary when they did something wrong. Then they would inform the parent about what happened. So, if you think you can misbehave just because your parents were not there, you need to think again. The idea of a community raising kids together was very real.

I was taught to enjoy the simple things in life and focus less on material things. I was taught to care for people around me and help them anyway I could. These are just few examples of the values that I grew up with.

So, when I showed up in America, I was psychologically ready to strive and get to where I wanted to be. The simple fact that I was able to come to the United States of America is already a success on its own. It is a success even if I were a street cleaner, a fry cook, or any other job some people in America might considered not too important.

Like I mentioned earlier, the political system, the government, and Institutions in my native country are widely considered tangled. So far, my home country has failed to enable a society that it citizens could be proud of. However, the cultural values that I and many from my native country were taught laid personal foundations for us. It's why we fight so hard. Our background is why we are so resilient to achieve more once we have the opportunity. And I believe this is true for many immigrants.

Resilience, hope, sharing, understanding, the notion of community, respect of others, and acceptance are a few of the traits engraved in me at very young age. They are my foundation and guide me along the way.

How I Learned English

You may have heard: English is a difficult language to learn.

For someone who never truly formed a full sentence in English before landing in America, learning English was a real challenge. In fact, I am still learning English 14 years later. Even though English was taught in school back in Togo, I took it seriously only after I landed in America.

American novelist and physician Khaled Hosseini said "if culture is a house, then language is the key to the front door; to all the rooms inside. Without it," he said, "you ended up wayward, without a proper home or a legitimate identity."

I can't emphasize enough how true this statement is. I look at how far I have come in my journey to be where I am today. The ability to communicate properly in any culture, in my opinion, is the key to access that culture. Every time we speak, we tell the world who we are and how we view things.

Learning a new language is not always easy. Some argue that children can readily absorb any language they find in their environments. They say children can quickly be fluent in a new language compared to adults. During my Army career however, I encountered many service members who learned foreign languages at great speed. Whichever side you are on in this debate, the beginning is always challenging.

Over the years I encountered people from various communities who lived in the U.S. for over 10 years. And yet when they speak English, I wondered about their slow and stumbling progress.

Later, I understood their limitations better. Embarrassments are inevitable. Misunderstandings are built in. You will be embarrassed at least a few times trying to have a simple conversation. You will say the wrong thing to the right person. You will get on the wrong bus because you could not properly read instructions. You will order the wrong food. All this will make an immigrant resort to hanging out with your "own kind", meaning people who speak their native language.

As I mentioned, I grew up in a French-speaking country. English was not very high on my list of languages to learn. Basic English was taught in middle school and high school in Togo. But I never took it seriously. And this explains how at age twenty-four I found myself unable to spell my own name, count one to ten, or say the complete alphabet in English. Nevertheless, I was resolved to learn.

I remembered watching TV programs designed for children on PBS Kids. I would get my sketchpad out and turn on Sesame Street, Barney and Friends, or Arthur. I took notes and began doing more research on words I could not understand. This experience turned out to be phenomenal. Since these programs were designed for children, they provided me with basic explanations of concepts, words, pronunciations, social norms, and acceptable and unacceptable behaviors in the American social culture. I believe today that education programs for children are the reflection of society values and norms in any country. So, the next time you travel anywhere, and you want learn about the culture, watch what they teach their children.

Then, I watched local and national news channels. These helped me learn how to speak proper English before I went to school. Most journalists and their guests are college graduates in various fields. They provided me with a vast intellectual vocabulary bank. With the twenty-four-hour news cycle, I had the opportunity to hear things over and over again. On top of the helpful repetition, news images reinforced my understanding of the stories I was hearing.

In addition to expanding my vocabulary, I learned a great deal about the American political system from watching the news between August and November, 2004. That was an exciting election year with George W. Bush and John Kerry on the ballot.

Next, I signed up for a free membership at the Laurel Public Library. I was able to check out English-as-a-second-language books and audio tapes. Other materials were also available for first-time English learners.

What surprised me the most during this time was the free library membership. You might find this statement a little bizarre. Let me explain. In Togo's education system, most of our textbooks were outdated versions from the 1950s, '60s, and '70s. The discipline we received in school prepared most Africans you might come across to excel in the American school system, but we read and studied things that were not really appropriate to our time. And we certainly did not have a free library system back in Togo. Even if they had existed during my time in school, you would not find current books, audios, videos or materials to check out and use for free.

During my college years in Togo, as a law student, I had to make paid copies of the textbook we were supposed to use. And there was no usable material in the college library. So, the vast amount of materials available for free in the U.S. public libraries here was mind blowing. This specific library in Laurel, Maryland quickly became my favorite place.

There I studied all day, surfed the internet for free (I had to pay for internet surfing in Togo), researched many topics, and tracked down English versions of books I had read before in French. I compared English and French books side by side. This technique sped up my learning process. My favorite book to do a comparison on, believe it or not, was the Bible. Because I had grown up going to church with my family, listening to sermons and reading the Bible myself, I was familiar with many chapters in French and Ewe (my native language).

Now that I was learning English, I chose familiar biblical chapters and tried to read them in my new language. My mind already knew the meaning of what I was reading, so I was just memorizing the English version. This technique also revealed to me quickly that not everything could be translated word for word from French to English.

In a very short time I learned how to respond appropriately to greetings. With my concentrated studying, I could soon ask basic questions about time, locations, everyday life things, and so on. I made progress. But my progress included both successes and failures.

Restaurant Difficulties

I remembered when I went to a restaurant for the first time. I didn't know that "entrée menu" in America was the main meal and an appetizer was the starter dish. So, I ordered by pointing at items in the entrée menu, not knowing really what I was ordering.

You should have seen my face when they brought me two full plates plus an appetizer. In French, "entrée" means a dish served before the main course of a meal. There was my confusion. When I was asked what I wanted to drink, I just pointed to "sparkling water", thinking that I was asking for regular water. When I drank it, I almost spit it all out due to its unusual taste.

To prevent this kind of embarrassment, for long time, I avoided going to restaurants. Then I only went with someone who could translate to me in French. Later, I would order the same thing anytime I go back to that restaurant, just because I knew what to expect.

Subtle Meanings

Often, we do not realize that words have powerful meanings. We tend to use words casually. This is especially true if you are limited in vocabulary which was my case. Saying the right things at the right time and place were make or break moments for me when I was learning English. For instance, I remembered telling a friend she was "sexy and hot". What I meant to say was that she looked beautiful. You can imagine the expression on her face.

Skate vs stake, chicken vs kitchen, cereal vs serial, beach vs b*tches and many others were words I often mispronounced and misused. People were puzzled about what I meant. I also remembered being confused about terms like baby shower, homecoming and chick. There are many things to learn.

Since most of my language education occurred watching TV shows and programs, you can tell what I have been watching based on my rare conversations. Early on either it was profanity filled or misuse of words I didn't fully understand.

The first time I used the "f..." word was to describe chicken that

I was tired of eating. My friend gently cut me off and told me that was not an appropriate word to use. He proceeded to explain to me the various circumstances people use this word. He ended the conversation telling me that I really needed to comprehend the context when using my new vocabulary.

The bottom line is I immersed myself in learning American English. Although I made many embarrassing errors, my plunge into American life helped me understand the culture and eventually navigate it successfully.

More Adjustments

Prior to coming to the United States, I never gave any real thought to how I would adjust to a culture that was very different from Togo. I thought vaguely that it couldn't be that difficult. However, it wasn't simple. A normal gesture on my home continent could give a total opposite effect in the U.S.

For example, in Togo it is considered disrespectful to look into the eyes of someone older than you when talking to them. In America, talking to someone and not looking into their eyes means you are lying, shy or hiding something. I found this out years later. I had to learn so many small things to adapt and adjust properly.

And after a few trials, I also began using people's first name (no matter their age) while buying food, filling out forms, making friends, and so on.

Adjusting to life in the United States wasn't very difficult for me compared to other immigrants. I wanted to be in America so badly, I was ready for anything. As I look back, I realized that what made it easier for me was the fact that I was ready to leave my life in Togo behind. I saw change as a good thing for me and my future. I did everything in my power to integrate with the culture. Above all I remained open minded. I was always willing to consider different options.

However, I couldn't say that I didn't have homesickness and cultural shock my first year. American culture is unique is many ways; and it is very difficult to portray it in a simply. What is acceptable in New York or the East Coast in general might not be acceptable when you go to North Carolina or the South, for example.

Regional Differences

I lived in the Washington, D.C. metro area the first 4 years of my life in America. I noticed that people "keep to themselves" in public areas such as metro or bus stations. I remembered one morning standing at the bus stop waiting for my bus to arrive. There was another gentleman standing not too far away. Just out of courtesy, I walked up to him and greeted him. I wanted to ask him if he had been standing there for a while. As I said good morning, he barely looked at me with an icy facial expression. He responded coldly. A soon as I began talking, he just walked away from me while murmuring something I didn't catch.

Later I recounted the "incident" to my cousin; and he told me that was typically the case. People do not just talk to strangers. I founded it a little shocking. Where I grew up, it didn't matter if you know the person or not, you are friendly. You can politely greet each other and strike up a conversation.

After this incident, I became a cultural detective. I began paying attention to people's behaviors anytime I waited for a bus or metro. And remarkably, I noticed that everyone was in their "head". I would see two people, for example, standing not even ten feet away from each other and will not speak or engage in any conversation.

Everyone seemed to be busy or preoccupied by something. I found this very strange. But gradually I accepted that this was the norm. And soon after my observations I adopted the same behavior.

But customs vary in other parts of the United States. When I moved to North Carolina, this type of "keeping to yourself" behavior was not the norm. I quickly noticed that people are much friendlier than I experienced up North.

When I moved into my first house in the community right outside the city of Greensboro, I recalled driving by and neighbors waiving friendly hellos. The first time this happened, my impression was "what is wrong here"? Why are people waving, I asked myself? I discovered later that people in the South are generally eager to engage in conversation even with a total stranger. They will say hello or the greeting of the day to whomever they happen to cross.

I remember the first week of my move when I was mowing my yard. Ms. King, a retired lady who lived next door, came by. She introduced herself and told me all I needed to know about the neighborhood I just moved to. She was very friendly and generous. She offered me a list of repair contractors she used for anything you can think of as homeowner.

Ms. King is a North Carolina native who lived her entire life in the state. She told me countless stories about people who lived in the neighborhood. She talked about what was life like for her growing up in the South. When she found out that I was born and raised far away from North Carolina she explained even more. We had numerous talks about our country's painful past of slavery and racial discrimination.

And every time we discussed these very sensitive topics, it reminds me of how much was accomplished by previous and current generations in the fight of social justice for all. Without this progress,

I am sure I would not have had the opportunities I have now. Yes, a lot was done. And there is more progress to go; and that is what America is about. There is constant questioning of who we are and what we can do differently to better the lives of future generations. This again is one reason the United States of America is so different and unique compared to any other country.

Peoples' attitudes vary from location to location inside the U.S. As immigrants we do not know this before coming, so it took me a little time to adjust.

Another cultural shock was the first time I saw two men kissing in the DuPont Circle area of Washington, D.C. I came from a very conservative society. I only heard of gays and lesbians through the media. I had never actually seen or met any in person. I remembered asking my friend if the police would arrest them for doing such a thing in public. My friend has been in the U.S. for much longer. She laughed at me and told me, "listen, this is the land of the free, and the home of the braves. No one is going to jail because they are holding hands, or kissing."

The Parties

As far as social life was concerned, in my first years, I went exclusively to African events. Holidays, birthdays and graduations parties with other immigrants was just where I felt comfortable at first.

Most Africans you meet in the United States always call another Africans their 'brother" or their "sister". We all are from the same continent. We are all brothers and sisters from the same motherland. This camaraderie is core to the African community. That is why every time there is any African party, you will find people from other countries in Africa regardless of whether the party host is from

Ghana, Togo, Kenya or another country.

A typical African party will have food and unlimited drinks. Parties are guaranteed to include spirited African music, generally the top hits of African songs which always send the crowd wild. When I said African music and songs, I am referring to all music put together. As you know, Africa is home for one billion people. It has 54 different countries and thousands of different languages and cultures. So, the music varies a lot from region to region and country to country.

As my English improved and my cultural understandings increased I gradually ventured out to different nightlife experiences. I worked on integrating myself with my new country. I began frequenting establishments with mixed crowds to include Caucasian, African-American, Jamaicans, and Latinos into my new life.

CHAPTER 5:
From Popeye's to the Pentagon

The road to success is not straight. It is bumpy, it is hard, it is
complicated, but is worth it.   -Unknown

From my arrival in the United States to my present employment, I had countless jobs. As I tell you about them here, I don't want you to focus on the jobs themselves. Look at the path they took me down. Our journeys take us to where we want to be; but the lines are never straight. Embrace where you are today. And never stop learning new skills that will take you to your destination.

Unless your parents name you the chief executive officer of their own company right out of high school or college, you will have to start at the bottom of the economic ladder and then climb your way to the top. The American economic system is a steep scramble. You start on the low rung with minimum wage. Years later you could be earning a six- or seven-figure income. It is possible, and the key is to become more and more valuable to the marketplace.

The bottom of the ladder was where I found myself in 2004, when I came to this country. I started off earning perhaps thirteen thousand a year. And a little over a decade later I crossed the six-figure income mark. How was this possible? The answer is simple: I changed. I became more valuable to the marketplace by learning new, in-demand skills. Here is how I started.

Popeye's Fast-Food Restaurant

At the age of twenty-four, my very first job in the United States of America was a fry cook at Popeye's. My cousin, with whom I was staying at the time, worked for the restaurant before. And when I arrived he asked the store manager if they were hiring. The store manager replied that their cook had resigned a couple weeks ago, and they needed a replacement.

I can't describe how happy I was to get this job. I worked six days a week, eight to twelve hours a day. I took such pride in this job. And every time someone called out, I was the first to volunteer to pick up those shifts. I was earning $6.25 per hour.

Bellman/Bellhop at the Sofitel & Willard Intercontinental Hotel

As I became more proficient in English, I was hired as a bellhop at Sofitel Hotel in Washington, D.C., in October, 2005. This was the most fun job for me. I assisted guests with their luggage and suggested restaurants, popular places to visit, and fun things to do while they were in town. All this was done with a smile and a positive attitude.

At first, I was shy. I had never worked in a luxurious hotel or been exposed to guests who came from the upper end of society. This job helped me build my self-confidence in dealing with people—some pleasant and some not-so-much. I was making $8 dollars an hour plus tips. This was a big improvement from my first restaurant job; and I made some great friends with whom I am still in contact to this day.

After working at the Sofitel Hotel for little over a year, I got my second job as bellhop at the Willard Inter-Continental Hotels in

Washington, D.C. Between my two jobs I worked almost every day. I was focused on saving money to start college.

First College Experience in the U.S.

I began college in the spring of 2007 at Montgomery Community College in Takoma Park, Maryland. The first time I walked into the classroom, I couldn't help but compare it to the University of Lomé, where I had studied last. At this community college, I had access to everything I needed to be a successful student: small classroom sizes, books, libraries, computer labs, and any other resource I could think of. What luxury!

In contrast, the University of Lomé in Togo lacked decent classrooms, proper study materials, and even seats in the classrooms. For example, when I was a law student, I had to arrive at my 8:00 a.m. class by 5:30 a.m. to have a chance of finding a decent seat. Some students came to class as early as 4:30 a.m. There were at least 500 students inside a 200-seat, amphitheater-style building. Another issue was the nonexistent study materials, dated books, and lack of practical application of anything that was taught. On top of these difficulties, professors were not paid regularly. So, they often went on strike to make their voices heard.

As I entered the American education system, I was relieved that I did not have to deal with any of those problems. I could finally pursue my education. However, I was faced with another reality: money for college.

The savings I accumulated before starting school dwindled quickly when I paid for my tuition, books, and living expenses. I worked two minimum wage jobs, paid for school out of pocket and paid for my rent and various expenses. I was not qualified for federal grants or loans. After two semesters at Montgomery Community College, I dropped out of school simply because I couldn't afford it anymore.

The decision to drop out was a very painful. I had dreamed so much about finishing my education. But I promised myself that I would return. My plan was to work six months to pay for one semester every year until I graduated. But living in the Washington, D.C., area on minimum wage was a challenge. I could barely pay rent and other living expenses—much less college tuition—by working two jobs.

Soon, a friend of mine who lived in Louisville, Kentucky, shared with me how low the cost of living was. He also told me how easy it was to get decent-paying jobs in his state. I visited him. A few months later I decided to move to Louisville, thinking this move could help me achieve my goal.

Galt House Hotel in Louisville, Kentucky

I arrived in Louisville in the summer of 2008. I immediately applied for a customer service job at the Galt House Hotel. Thanks to my previous experience as a bellhop, I was hired on the spot.

With 1,300 guest rooms, Galt House Hotel is the largest hotel in Kentucky. This was a busy place, and I fit right in. After working there for about six months, I was ready to return to college. However, I couldn't get a work schedule that was compatible with the classes I wanted to take. I needed a job with much more flexibility. A friend of mine who was a taxicab driver suggested that I try driving, as well. I had never driven a taxi before, but since my priority was to return to school, I applied for a taxicab license with a company called Ready Cab.

Taxi Driver in Louisville, Kentucky

Being a taxi driver was very interesting. I was my own boss. I woke up when I wanted too, worked whenever I felt like it, and attended Jefferson Community College in Louisville, Kentucky. I took classes in the morning. Once I was done, I got on the road. This schedule flexibility allowed me to work and attend classes at the same time, but it wasn't easy. My days were ten to fifteen hours long.

Downtown Louisville—and especially Fourth Street—was the main area to find customers, so that was my staging area. Fourth Street was the entertainment district, filled with bars and restaurants right in the heart of downtown Louisville. It was a perfect place to find customers on weekends. I spent most of my time down there, in front of hotels, nightclubs, bars, and museums.

But the biggest business opportunity for taxi drivers in Louisville was during the Kentucky Derby. Once a year, on the first weekend of May, people come from all over the world to attend horse racing. (This time is also known as "the most famous four minutes in sports".)

The race itself is not the most important thing about Derby. The event is famous for the festive ambiance that permeates the city from Thursday through Sunday. It is a city-wide party that crowds the streets, hotels, restaurants, and bars. During this time business opportunities were everywhere for taxi drivers. On Derby weekends, I worked with very little rest, earning three months of income in four days. I used the money to pay for tuition and books for the following semester. I did this two years in a row, until I decided to move to Greensboro, North Carolina in June, 2010.

Labor Worker in Greensboro, North Carolina

When I moved to Greensboro, North Carolina, I went to a temporary agency for a job. I was placed in a printing company that needed someone on the night shift. There I worked twelve hours a day, six days a week. I was what was known as a "floater," which basically meant I assisted wherever I was needed.

My company printed coupons for the grocery chain Food Lion. Some of my duties were: load and unload items from machines and conveyors, lift both raw materials and finished products, and pack items manually or using hoists. I was also responsible to observe equipment operations. If malfunctions were detected, I notified supervisors or machine operators. Other duties also included pushing, pulling and moving pallets with a pallet jack. I loaded and unloaded trucks, examined the printed products to verify conformance to quality standards and maintained a safe, organized and clean work area at all times.

I did this the next four months, earning $7.45 per hour. I was always tired coming home from this job. And I never had enough money to do anything even though I worked sixty hours a week. My future wasn't looking good. Around this time, I realized that my life wasn't going in the direction I wanted to. That's when I committed to my decision to join the U.S. Army.

College Years and Graduation in Greensboro, North Carolina

I joined the Army Reserve on October 1, 2010. It was the best decision of my life. I left for basic training and advanced individual training in November, 2010. I returned home in April, 2011.

This was when my life really began to improve. Once I returned home, I went back to school with a clear plan to pay my way through college. I used the Army GI bill and Tuition Assistance program (education benefits) to pay for my tuition and books. I also had monthly income for the following three years of college.

I also worked part time as a bellhop for O'Henry & Proximity Hotels in Greensboro. So, I was a full-time student taking between fifteen and twenty-one credits a semester, working part-time, and attending Army Reserve monthly training. I was always busy and never had time to relax, but I knew that every sacrifice I was making had a purpose.

In May, 2013 I graduated from North Carolina Agricultural & Technical State University with a bachelor's degree in international relations. I was over the moon when I walked across that stage to receive my diploma!

Thirteen years after I graduated from high school in my native country of Togo, and six years after I dropped out of Montgomery Community College in Maryland, I finally achieved my lifelong dream of graduating from college, all thanks to the United States Army.

Post College

After my graduation, I had the opportunity to work for my Army Unit Headquarters in Fort Bragg, North Carolina. I learned new skills that had nothing to do with my college degree, but I was eager to learn and adapt. I began training and applying new lessons in Information Technology. My open-minded attitude unlocked new doors for my career and allowed me to climb the social and professional ladder. I went from working at Fort Bragg to deployment in Djibouti and various other east African countries.

My First Deployment: Djibouti, Africa (2014 -2015)

I left the African continent as a Togolese citizen on March 23, 2004. Ten years later, on October 9, 2014, I arrived to Djibouti in East Africa as a U.S. citizen serving in the United States Army Civil Affairs and Psychological Operations Command. Never in my wildest dreams did I think this would even be possible for me. However, I landed in Djibouti, East Africa as an American soldier.

One of the things Africa is known for is its heat; and the weather in Djibouti confirmed its reputation. A former French Colony, the Republic of Djibouti is a country located in the Horn of Africa, with a population close to one million. The majority are Muslim. Close to the Red Sea, Djibouti is a hub of multinational maritime companies and multiple foreign military bases.

Everything seemed surreal to me. When our plane landed on the tarmac of Djibouti International Airport after almost 24 hours of travel, it was just past 6:00 a.m. local time on October 9, 2014. My teammates and I were all tired and needed to eat some real food. However, there were procedures and requirements to follow. We did the best we could to get through them as quickly as possible.

For the next nine months, I was assigned to Camp Lemonier, the only permanent U.S. military base on the African Continent.

I will remember my time in Djibouti for the rest of my life. I learned so many valuable lessons from my fellow soldiers, airmen, sailors, marines, and the international partners, military and civilians alike. I got the opportunity to travel to many other countries during this deployment, including Burundi, Kenya, Ethiopia, Tanzania, and others.

Life in this small, yet very busy base in Djibouti was very interesting. At first, just like anyone else, I struggled to find places on the base. It took a while to find the dining facility, the gym, and the "convenience store." But fortunately, the military installation was small, and I learned my way around.

Living Conditions

The living quarters I occupied were called CLUs (Containerized

Living Units). Basically, CLUs are forty-foot shipping containers made into apartments that house four people. A wall down the middle divides each container into two twenty-foot units that house two people each.

The area where we all lived was called CLU Ville (cleverly pronounced like "Whoville"). People who spend too much time in their quarters are were known as CLUsers (cleverly, but less kindly, pronounced like "losers").

The bathrooms, known as "ablutions," were peppered throughout CLU Ville. These were also forty-foot shipping containers, but they were filled with toilets at one end and showers and sinks at the other. The showers were only two feet by two feet. I couldn't put both of my elbows out without touching the walls.

Due to overcrowding on the base and the limited ability to process wastewater, we took combat showers. This meant turning on the water for thirty seconds to get wet, then turning off the water to lather up, and then turning it back on to rinse for no more than two-and-a-half minutes.

If we got greedy with the water, leadership would close the bathrooms and limit our access.

Djibouti was very hot, so it was imperative that people washed their clothes. Under normal circumstances, we could either wash our own laundry in CLU Ville or drop it off and have it done for us. Both had advantages. But water conservation also made laundry a challenge. When there was a shortage that meant no clean laundry— and lots of odor.

Amenities

Camp wasn't anything fancy, but it wasn't all combat showers and

CLUs, either. If we could handle the heat moving from one building to another, we had everything we needed right there at base.

Food in the camp was served primarily in the dining facilities, which we called chow halls. Subway was available while I was there, and Pizza Hut opened right after I left. Most meals were typical cafeteria food—Monday's meatloaf became Tuesday's sloppy Joe. But they did a good job of providing variety and adding some ethnic foods like Mexican, Chinese, or Filipino to keep it interesting. We could get food 24/7, but sit-down meals were only available during certain hours. Otherwise, we got our food packaged to go.

For supplies, we could buy nearly anything we needed in the Navy Exchange (NEX). They may not have huge selections of preferred brands, but they had all the essentials and plenty of snacks.

The twenty-four-hour gym and 2.25-mile running trail provided ample exercise options. The camp offered yoga, martial arts, and sports for us as well.

We could get internet access in our rooms, but we had to pay a hefty price for it. (Most of us did—being able to communicate privately with our loved ones was worth the money.) But the "Green Bean Café," which was essentially a Starbucks, had free Wi-Fi access. And if we were interested in using the Wi-Fi for educational pursuits, the camp provided college classes and library services, too.

The recreation center, 11 Degrees North, had pool, darts and ping-pong, as well as nighttime entertainment including karaoke and DJs. The big outdoor stage and huge patio made it a great place to hang out.

Finally, we are allowed two alcoholic beverages a day. (I don't drink, so I wasn't affected by that rule.) We could buy those drinks at 11 Degrees North or at The Old Cantina, which was a laid-back outdoor gathering place that had a reputation for being where the "older folks" hung out.

Not All Wi-Fi and Karaoke

Deployment life is one of the most challenging things service members and their families go through. Having to leave everyone and everything behind to go to these foreign places, and conduct our country's military business requires a lot of character and dedication. Many times, we rely on the internet to keep in touch with loved ones.

Talking to people who went on previous deployments in Iraq or Afghanistan, you realize that it depletes you. Many people confessed how relationships fell apart, kids grew up, or things happened during deployment that forever altered their lives. From an outsider's view, giving your life to your country might seem very simple, however this is not an easy life. It is like giving a blank check to someone and asking them to write any amount they desire and cash it. So, when I see countless people doing it with passion, I am always humbled by their commitment.

Inspiring Leaders

During my time in Djibouti, I had the privilege of working with and for unique people. Many of them inspired me because of their life stories, their work ethic, their dedication, and their inner strength. I am proud to have met and learned from these talented and unique individuals:

Major General Wayne Grigsby (U.S. Army): Commander of the Combined Joint Task Force Horn of Africa.

Growing up in Togo, I saw army officers behave selfishly due to their ranks and positions. But I learned swiftly that in the U.S. Armed Forces being an officer was not about you but about your country and your soldiers. General Grigsby personified that caring.

First of all, it is a unique privilege to any non-commissioned officer or junior officer to be in the presence of a two-star general. When Major General Grigsby wanted to administer my Oath of Office, I just couldn't believe that top U.S. Army General on the African continent would take time out of his busy schedule to induct someone like me.

General Grigsby always had a word of encouragement and appreciation every time he saw a group of soldiers. He made sure you knew that whatever your job was, you were important to the overall mission. He was always present at sporting events, early morning runs, physical trainings, and many other small activities on post. I was truly honored to learn from this man what an officer should be.

Command Sergeant Major Bonnie Skinner (U.S. Marines Corps): The first time I met Command Sergeant Major Skinner was during the preparation to go on a mission to Burundi in November, 2014. She knew me for ten minutes when she made an important decision. Once Sgt. Maj. Skinner found out I spoke fluent French, she immediately told me to get ready for the mission with her.

Her instant trust in me made a very positive first impression. I wondered about such a quick decision without asking for more information about my background.

Later I asked her that question and she replied, "As a leader, Sergeant Afetse, many times you will have to make decisions based on the little information you have at your disposal. You'll need to trust your instinct."

Sgt. Maj. Skinner is a professional and a compassionate leader; but you don't want to cross her. She is known for her remarkable discipline. Even though she's quick to acknowledge a soldier for his or her efforts, she will not shy from calling someone out if he/she "messed up."

During our trip to Burundi, I was fortunate to see her in action at the Non-Commission Officer Academy. She was received with such admiration and enthusiasm everywhere we went. She spoke eloquently at the Non-Commissioned Officers Academy and at the U.S. Marines Corps ball organized by the U.S. Embassy in Burundi.

When I informed Sgt. Maj. Skinner that I had received my commission as a 2nd Lieutenant, she was thrilled for me. She even organized a reception in my honor after my oath of office. Her office sent out invitations to various offices on camp to attend this ceremony. I was truly at a loss for words to thank her for all she did. She was an exemplary leader whose tenure in Djibouti showed how a Senior Non-Commissioned Officer can lead and inspire soldiers, marines, airmen, and sailors. I am truly thankful to have met her.

Staff Sergeant Rachel Julien (U.S. Army): SSG Julien was in charge of accountability for newly arrived service members in Djibouti. She performed consistent, high-quality work, which I believe will take her to higher assignments in her career. She went above and beyond to assist service members who needed help. She always followed up to be sure any issue that had been brought up to her had been resolved.

She remembered her teammates' birthdays and other special occasions; and she always came up with initiatives to celebrate these events in or out of the office. She strongly valued her heritage from Trinidad and never missed the opportunity to share Caribbean culture with us. I will always remember her as someone who was confident, capable, creative, generous, and kind.

Staff Sergeant Will Buxton (U.S. Marines Corps): One word comes to mind whenever I think about this U.S. Marines Corps Staff Sergeant: integrity.

When I found out that I was going to be sharing my CLU with another branch member, I didn't know what to expect. I heard so many stories from experienced people about how deployment can be great or miserable depending on who you are housed with. But SSG Buxton was the best roommate I ever had. He taught me many lessons without even knowing it. The big one was integrity. I observed him quite a bit, and I admired the way he carried himself throughout deployment.

For instance, one night after a long day, I was lying in my bed watching TV before I fell into sleep. Around 11:00 p.m., Staff Sergeant Buxton, who had gone to sleep earlier, woke up and put on his uniform. I thought he must be going to work that night, so I was surprised when he returned fifteen minutes later with a Subway sandwich in his hand. I asked why he put on his uniform at 11:00 p.m. if he wasn't going to work, and he told me he was hungry and wanted a sandwich. Seeing my confusion, he smiled and told me about the Marines Corps Rules about uniform on base.

Now, our CLU was less than 100 feet from the Subway, it was after 11:00 p.m., and Buxton woke up starving. How many people would have ignored the rules and just run to get what they needed? Instead, Buxton had enough honor to do the right thing, even when nobody would've noticed him breaking the rules.

Buxton was disciplined and dedicated to his personal principles and the values of the Marines Corps. If he was not reading at night before going to sleep, he was talking to his family. He woke up early every morning to mentor fellow marines in his martial arts program, and he did CrossFit and every other sport I can think of.

One of the seven Army values is integrity, and it is defined as "doing the right thing when no one is looking." SSG Buxton truly lived by this value, so when I heard he was selected to become an officer, I couldn't be any prouder of him. He rightly deserved that next level of leadership. He was definitely going places, and I am glad I could call him my friend.

Lieutenant Colonel Richard Sonnenfeld (U.S. Army): My one word for LTC Sonnenfeld is enthusiasm. I am pretty sure everyone who has met or worked with LTC Sonnenfeld will tell you this guy was a dedicated officer. The first time I met him was during my first trip to Burundi, when he was working at the U.S. Embassy. He was full of energy and very passionate about his job, pouring his heart into whatever he was doing. His zest and enthusiasm were contagious. People like LTC Richard Sonnenfeld are the ones keeping our Army organization alive through their devotion and dedication. I am very thankful to have known this great officer.

Major Isaac "Ike" Bradlich (U.S. Army): Commitment. Major Bradlich was the liaison officer for the Combined Joint Task Force in Burundi. He never showed his frustration with anyone or anything. Major Bradlich would keep a smile on his face even when nothing was going according to plan. He always remained composed and focused on what needed to be done. I was very impressed by his confidence and attitude.

Colonel Todd Fox (U.S. Army): No-Nonsense. During my duty as desk non-commissioned officer for Burundi, I attended many briefings and meetings. It was during one of these briefings that I saw Col. Fox in action. Everybody in the Combined Joint Task Force Horn of Africa knew that Colonel Fox was a no-nonsense guy. Colonel Fox was a very intelligent and articulate officer. He knew what needed to be done, and he would not tolerate shortcuts. If you didn't know your facts well, you knew to stay away from Colonel Fox, because there was no BSing this officer. I am glad that this kind of officer is part of our army.

Colonel Connors (U.S. Army): Visionary. Colonel Connors was the commander of the section I was assigned to during my deployment. He created the section right before my team arrived in Djibouti. One thing I learned from him was that, as a leader, you must have a vision. Colonel Connors knew where he wanted our section to go and knew how to communicate that to all of us. He was very approachable and did not look down on any soldier based on rank. He treated everyone with respect.

I had the opportunity to work with too many wonderful people to describe in detail here. These are a few of the others I'd like to recognize:
-Sergeant First Class Christopher Ifill, US Army
-Petty Officer Tachrece Barton, US Navy
-Sergeant Carina Reeve, British Army
-Petty Officer Alejandrina Rosser, US Navy
-Staff Sergeant Jessica Wolter, US Air Force,
-Commander Tom Radich, US Navy
-Ensign Danny Theis, US Navy
-Chief Demetrius O'Halloran, US Navy
-Chief William Jones, US Navy
-Master Sergeant Velma Wynn, US Air Force
-Staff Sergeant Ian Dean, US Air Force
-Command Sergeant Major Claudell Taylor, US Army,
-Lieutenant Colonel Joyce Craig, US Army
-Lieutenant Colonel David Noteboom, US Army
-Lieutenant Colonel Jared Cleary, US Army
-Colonel April Thomas, US Army

-Sergeant Jamie Zierwick, US Army

-Staff Sergeant Kelly Rakus, US Army

-Sergeant Paul Labbe, US Air Force

-Sergeant First Class Godwin Barely, US Army

-Staff Sergeant Alexander To, US Army

-Staff Sergeant Manis, US Army

-Staff Sergeant Zielinski, US Air Force.

To all of you who impacted my life and experience in Africa one way or another, even if I failed to name you here, I say thank you. May God keep you safe in your service to our nation, wherever you are. We might never cross paths again, but this chapter is dedicated to you, and I thank you for your service.

Department of State

During my deployment in Djibouti a friend of mine told me about job opportunities at the State Department in Washington D.C. He informed me that he was working for the State Department on a contractual basis. He could recommend me if I wanted to work there, since I had the required qualifications. I told him that working for the State Department had been my dream, and that I would be very grateful if he could recommend me. He did, and once we returned to the U.S., I began my new work there.

I devoted myself to my job at the State Department, but I never stopped looking for better opportunities, learning new skills, studying, and exploring new fields of learning so I could be better at whatever I did. I had taken various classes in information technology, and I worked to deepen my learning in this field. This way of thinking and doing things opened me up to better opportunities and helped me keep moving upward.

The Pentagon

I could have been content with my climb from a fast food kitchen to the State Department; however, I still believed I could do more.

By now I had many qualifications from my education, my experience in the army, and life in general. The job at the State Department required that I learn a new set of skills. To get to the next level, I still had to keep learning.

Busy as I was working full time, traveling, and taking care of my family, I devoted my spare time to learning more critical skills the market was seeking. Since success is opportunity meeting preparedness, I finally got my new position at the Pentagon. With that my soul felt like there were really no limits to where I could go and what I could do.

I know my readers would like more details about my Pentagon work, but for security reasons, I must be brief and vague.

As you can see, I made a decision from the very beginning not to stand still in my professional or personal life. In my story, the results confirm that the application of certain mind-sets or life principles will undeniably yield the expected result.

In the second part of this book, I will explain the principles I used—and still use—to get to anything I truly desired. I did not invent any of these principles; in fact, they have been around forever.

My search for answers to life's big questions led me to these laws, and when I applied them, they changed my experience on this earth. I hope they will do the same for you.

PART II: **The Principles**

Along my journey, I learned and applied many principles that I would like to share with you.

Unexpected Inspiration

Jim Rohn, one of the great leaders in the field of personal development, said, "Things don't just happen, they happen just." Who knew that a simple trip to a thrift store not far from where I lived in Silver Spring, Maryland, could be a life-changing event?

I went to this store one April morning in 2005 for no specific reason. While I was browsing through the electronics aisle, I came across my very first personal development audiobook: Tracy Brian's The Psychology of Achievement. I took the cassette tapes home, and from the moment I listened to them for the first time, I knew my life would never be the same. This audiobook opened the gates for a new way of thinking and taught me a new, concrete approach to changing my life. The most surprising thing about it? This life-changing knowledge cost me only four dollars.

In my quest for a better life, I read and studied the works of many experts in human development. Among them are Earl Nightingale, Jim Rohn, Brian Tracy, Denis Waitley, Zig Ziglar, Les Brown, Tony Robbins, and many others. I did my best to give all of them credit throughout this book.

These people are the mentors who unknowingly helped me set and achieve all my goals. Now I am paying their favor forward to anyone who will read these lines—today or many years from now.

In this book, I have mentioned many principles and laws of the universe. I also discuss how their application can transform our lives. However, I didn't invent any of these ideas and principles; I simply took possession and applied them to my life to get the results I am enjoying today.

I hope my story sparks or strengthens your desire to live your life your way.

I hope Part II of this book and my story will encourage you to reach deeper inside of yourself and go after what you truly want.

My heartfelt and sincere thanks to anyone who has been and continues to be a positive influence in my life.

Part II continues my story and my experience coming to the United States and becoming an American citizen. I have strong, positive feelings for this great nation, and some might not share those feelings for reasons connected to politics, military activity, or social injustice. I can respect that. I embrace the difference in opinions, and I challenge everyone to do their part to make this great nation better.

CHAPTER 6
Principle 1: Your Attitude and Philosophy

A positive attitude from you tends to produce a positive attitude
toward you. —Deborah Day

Looking back at my youth, I picture a very optimistic person dreaming about what I wanted out of life. I always dreamed of becoming someone who could impact people positively—even though I didn't have a clue about how. I am not sure where I got that idea. Even as a child I was always the first to offer an alternative when my friends and I found ourselves in a situation that looked doomed. My attitude and philosophy toward life was "There is a better situation somewhere, and it is my job to find it." I believe my hope and optimism allowed me to overcome many challenges I faced and am still facing.

Your attitude can be defined as the way you feel about people and situations you encounter. First, let me ask you this question: what is your attitude toward life? What is your attitude toward people, events, or situations you face daily?

Philosopher and Psychologist William James said, "The greatest discovery of my generation is that human beings can change their lives by changing their attitudes of mind." Simply put, your attitude will determine life's attitude toward you! If you wake up expecting that your day will be great, no matter what happens, you are probably going to have a great day.

The same is true for the way you interact with people. If you decide not to let their negative moods or pessimistic views affect you, you are already a winner. Life is about cause and effect, whether you accept it or not. For every action, there is an equal reaction. Practically speaking, people will give back to you what you put out to them. If you've never thought about this before, I encourage you to take a step back and analyze your conception of life.

You control your attitude. When you wake up every morning, what is the first thing that comes into your mind? Do you say to yourself, "This is going to be a great day," or do you let your mind drag you to yesterday's problems, starting your day with negative feelings? If you remember that you're in control, and you're conscientious about the attitude you choose, you will have better days and a better life.

Very often we mistakenly think that other people control our reactions to various situations. For example, if you say good morning to a co-worker with a smile and get nothing in return, your immediate reaction may be to frown and think, "What is wrong with that person?" Or you may think, "What is wrong with me that my co-worker won't smile back?" If we think someone's nonresponse is our fault that is giving the other person control over our reactions. Doing that puts the other person in charge of how you respond to unpleasant situations. Take back your power.

Make a commitment to yourself today not to let other people's reactions affect your attitude toward them. Determine to control your feelings and emotions in every situation. Maintain your positive attitude. Every time you encounter an unpleasant person or situation, just remember to ask yourself this simple question: "Why would I let this person or situation control how I feel?"

Now I know there are tragic moments in life, like the death of a loved one or the sudden loss of a job. These moments demand a reaction. But these situations do not happen daily. The bottom line is that you must train your mind not to reply negatively to unpleasant events. The way to improve your attitude is to think first, then react.

Look for the "silver linings," or the positive lights in dark events. Train yourself to distinguish between things that are in your control and things that are not. Once you're good at this, I promise that you will be able to dramatically improve your reactions to unpleasant people and situations.

Is there someone in your life who is particularly good at thinking before reacting? Everybody needs a role model. So, my advice to you is to identify someone you'd like to emulate and learn as much as you can about that person. Find out how your role model became who he or she is and how he or she managed to overcome challenges.

I discovered many role models since I came to the United States. Among them is Jim Rohn, one of the great inspirational speakers of his generation. Even though he was born and raised in obscurity in southwest Idaho farm country, Rohn overcame educational, social, and financial limitations to create a well-defined life for himself and his family. And he inspired millions to do the same.

Your Philosophy About Life

Second, what is your philosophy? How do you conceive of life in general? What is your opinion of people? Do you think they are generally good or generally bad? Do you think you have your place in this world? Do you think you have control over your life, or is someone else in charge of you? Are you a prisoner of your own thoughts, or are you free from any kind of bondage?

Are you quick to judge people you've just met, or do you allow them to show you who they really are? What do you think about society in general? Do you think societal rules are rigged? Do you believe in hard work? How about taxes? Do you think the laws that govern society work against you, or do you think they are fair? How about our education system? How about religion? How about life and death?

I think you see where I am going with this. Maybe you thought about these big issues before, or maybe not. But the point I am trying to make is that your philosophy is what you know based on what you've heard from your parents, teachers, religious leaders, friends, the media, and so on. We all have our own philosophy of life, and my philosophy could be totally different from yours. That's what makes everyone unique. But it is crucial that you examine yours to know where you stand on these important life questions. Your philosophy will determine where you end up in your life. Make sure you are building a good foundation.

My personal philosophy is that life is two steps forward and one step back. This understanding has helped me see the bigger picture in every situation.

For example, disappointment is a part of life that we all experience. People we love will leave us or betray us. We'll fail to achieve things we really want, and achievements we've worked for years will suddenly become unsatisfying. No matter how high we climb, we will always want to climb higher.

I think people are genuinely good. However, everyone is selfish to an extent. Forget the idea that you can get something for free. Everybody wants something. There is no point in your life where you will get and say to yourself "now that I have arrived I can be happy". The bottom line is that life is a challenge, and it is constantly changing. There is no use looking for an easy life. If you refuse to see yourself as a victim of circumstance, and if you take responsibility for everything that happens to you, you'll find success and satisfaction are easier to come by.

I see myself as responsible for my own life's condition. Yes, I didn't choose the place of my birth or my parents, but I became responsible for my life somewhere along the way. I think my environment, my friends, my house, my car, my clothes, and my job are all reflections of my work and achievements.

So, take charge of yourself and everything in your life. Examine your attitude and your philosophy. Take time to think. Refuse to give anybody the power to make you mad or tell you to live by what they think.

Your attitude and philosophy toward life will determine where you go. Realize that you are in the driver's seat! Begin today with a new attitude. And watch how people mirror what you are putting out. If occasionally you come in contact with an unpleasant person or situation, shrug it off, and keep moving. Don't give in to their miseries; live your life your way.

CHAPTER 7
Goals and Your Imagination

Setting goals is the first step in turning the invisible into the visible.
—Tony Robbins

This is perhaps the most important chapter in this entire book. If you read this book and can only take away one thing, please pay attention to this chapter. Goal setting completely changed my life, enabling me to do more in a very short time than most people do in a lifetime.

One of the biggest failures of our school system is that you can go from kindergarten to a Ph.D. without ever receiving instruction on goal setting. This is true even though setting goals is vital to achieving anything in life. If you don't know what you want or where you want to go, it is very difficult—even downright impossible—to get there.

Until I arrived in the United States, I didn't know you could plan your life on paper. I didn't know that goal setting was a science you could use to make things happen for yourself, your family, or your company.

A lot of people live by what I call the "crossed fingers theory." They hope their way through life and go nowhere because they never take time to set proper goals. Not that hope is a bad thing in itself, but hope is not a strategy, and hope without any action is delusion.

When I began setting goals, my first concern was how to make whatever I had just written down a reality. You probably ask yourself the same question every time you think about doing something new. The answer is imagination and action! I will address this very shortly, but first let me tell you that your very first step to achieving anything is to know what you want and write it down.

Looking back on my past, I realized that I unknowingly used goal setting, imagination, and action to get the visa I needed to come to the United States. When I became fascinated with the United States of America, I was determined to find a way to get there. How was I going to do that? I had no idea.

Nevertheless, I wrote it down in my journal under "wishful thinking." From time to time I would go to my journal and fantasize about my dream. After I graduated from high school, I went to the U.S. Embassy to ask about requirements for traveling to United States. Then I went back to my journal and wrote down all the requirements for obtaining a visa. Long story short, I took action. And you know the rest of the story.

Since I hadn't realized back then that this was a strategy I could use methodically to get anything out of life, I went right back to my old ways of thinking and doing things. It would not be until that fateful morning in April, 2005 when I bought my first audiobook, Brian Tracy's "The Psychology of Achievement," that my eyes were opened to the importance of setting goals.

From then on I set goals: learning English, making better friends, getting a new job, obtaining American citizenship, earning a college degree, and saving money. I also wanted to have a family, be in good physical condition, buy my dream car, buy a house, become an Army officer, become an author… The list goes on. I have set goals for the next three, five, and ten years. I have goals for every month and year.

I am a great believer in setting goals. I know that writing your goals down and putting them where you can see them can make the difference between success and failure. To help me keep my personal goals in the forefront of my mind, I write them on small business cards and keep them in my wallet. I also keep them inside my car where I can see them. These simple cards keep my most important goals front and center.

When you have goals, life becomes very interesting. Here is what you need to do:

1. Decide who you want to be.

2. Sit down and make a complete, accurate analysis of your life. Where are you in your personal life, family, finances, career, love life, etc. Be completely honest with yourself. Write everything down.

3. Ask yourself these questions: If you had no limitations whatsoever, what would you be or do? Who do you want to share your life with? How much money do you need to make your life easier? Where do you see yourself working? The more specific details you write down on each topic the better. Don't worry about how all that will happen. Let yourself go and write everything down without worrying about how it will all happen.

4. Think about your life as a whole, as though you are the architect determining what finished building or house.

5. Prioritize everything on your list from the most important to the least important. This will help you identify which actions to take first and why. For example, if you want a better job you will probably need a degree, a certificate, or some form of training.

6. Create a plan. This plan can cover weeks, months, or years depending on what you are trying to achieve. For instance, if you want to learn a new language, your plan could be to buy Rosetta Stone and study one hour every Tuesday and Thursday.

7. Clearly define why you are setting these goals. Visual clarity is very powerful. The world's best athletes use visualization. It works.

8. Make a commitment to yourself to follow your plan.

Your goals will guide you through all of your life changes. Have you met a captain of any plane or ship who didn't know exactly where he or she was going next—or how to get there? It is impossible. The crew of every plane in the sky or a ship in the water can tell you their next destination without hesitation. You are the captain of your own life.

To go somewhere you must set that destination in mind, put it on paper, and commit to getting there. When I say goals, I don't mean daydreams. Goals are something you can work to achieve. Your goals are the guiding principles on which to build and achieve your future. If you have never set goals, this new knowledge will revolutionize your life.

You can never be successful or get anywhere in your life until you perfect goal setting, but the goals themselves aren't enough. You must divide everything by yearly goals, monthly objectives, weekly plans, and daily tasks. You must break your goals down into twenty-four-hour increments and look at how you spend your days. This includes your sleeping time, working time, driving time, and everything you do throughout the day.

Then, by incorporating a few disciplines into your daily routine, you can start to achieve your major goals. After all, as Lao Tzu said,

"The journey of a thousand miles begins with the first step."

Review your goals daily, weekly, and monthly to see your progression. Accept that there will be setbacks, disappointments, delays, and temporary defeats. But resolve to never give up.

Life is an up-and-down journey, so plan your comebacks. Carry yourself accordingly, and don't treat your temporary denials as permanent failures. Set goals that will challenge you, excite you, and motivate you.

Remember that you are not competing with anybody, so take time to create. Don't be in a rush—be patient, and let time take care of you. It is not enough to talk about your goals. You must have them in writing and develop a plan to achieve them. A goal without a plan is a mere wishful thinking.

Your better future is for you and your family to enjoy, but first you must create that future in your mind. Where do you want go? Want do you want to be? Without dreams and visions, people perish.

When you become a goal-oriented person, this doesn't mean that everybody around you will be supportive of what you are trying to achieve. On the contrary, your first battle to reach a new level will begin in your immediate surroundings. Self-doubts, negative relatives, cynical friends, and doubting co-workers will do their best to talk you out of whatever you come up with.

Focus on the big picture. Decide what you want. Accept the price you'll pay to achieve it. You'll have to make sacrifices, because you cannot be focused on a hundred things all the time.

Obsession, obsession, obsession! You must be obsessed with your goals and back your plan with faith and determination. Research people who have done what you are trying to do. Ask questions. Read books. Listen to programs about your goals. Be flexible yet firm. Adapt, overcome, and achieve.

Your Own Words

It is not what others said about you that matters, it is what you are saying about yourself. —Bishop T.J. Jakes

What you say about yourself is very powerful, so watch your words all the time, because they will become your reality. Never say anything negative or allow anybody to say negative things about you in your presence. (Anything said behind your back is irrelevant.)

Stay away from destructive criticism, since it doesn't help you. And keep your goals to yourself. We tend to think when we share our goals, others will hold us accountable and we'll be more likely to achieve. Derek Sivers says it's better to keep goals secret. He presents research stretching as far back as the 1920s to show why people who talk about their ambitions may be less likely to achieve them. So, just as the seed has to be buried in the ground in order to grow, your goals need to be protected against negative outside influences that will destroy them.

You are the company that you keep, so choose your friends carefully. Your circle of friends will influence you in either a positive or negative way. Stay away from negative mindsets. Just like you need healthy food to feed your body, you need healthy mental protein to feed your mind.

Your Actions

Setting goals is just one side of the coin. To make your goals bloom, you will need a plan and action. You can spend your time putting your goals on paper and writing very good plans; however, that's only part of the work. You need to act on your plans.

If your goal is to lose a certain amount of weight, and you have to a plan to go to the gym twice a week and eat healthy food, you're on the right track. But until you actually get inside the gym or learn to cook nutritious meals, nothing will be accomplished.

You can study your goal and your plan all day long, but you will never achieve your desired weight until you get moving. There is no way around it.

When I set my goal to become an army officer, I didn't even have a college degree. I knew I had to go back to college, register for classes, talk to advisors, buy school material, attend classes, do my homework, study, and take my tests semester after semester until I graduated. Then I had to look up the process for becoming an officer and choose my next steps based on where I was in life. There is no "one size fits all" when it comes to setting your goals and achieving them. You are obliged to design your own plan and act on it.

Dealing with Setbacks

During this process of going after your dreams, you will encounter pitfalls that you'll need to overcome if you are going to be successful.

The very first pitfall is that not everything you desire in your life will be yours. You are going to face challenges and difficulties. You will experience setbacks, rejections, and lots of temporary defeats. Don't be discouraged when these moments come. What you need to do is to back every single plan you have with persistence. Commit to never, ever giving up on your goals.

Your persistence reflects how much faith you have in your own ability to succeed. Things will not always go the way you want them to. Remember, you must stay the course if you truly believe in achieving your goals. It is fine to revise your plans and change your actions, but do not give up on your goals.

Lastly, every time you run into an impasse, go back to the reason you set the goal in the first place. This is the most powerful motivating force behind every goal you set for yourself. Why are you doing what you want to do? Why did you decide to graduate from college? Why did you decide to get a new job? Why did you want to get healthy? Why did you break off that relationship? Go back to that reason, and I can promise that you will find the strength to overcome any challenge that might come your way.

I cannot even recall how many times in my life I was turned down or told no, it couldn't be done, or I wasn't good enough. Had I listened to those people and quit, I don't think I would have the privilege to be talking to you right now.

For example, when I finished college and wanted to become an army officer, I talked to recruiter. I was excited about my goal, but after a brief discussion, the recruiter told me that it was no longer possible for me to go to Officer Candidate School. I was too old. When I asked him if there were any other way I could become an officer, he told me it was unfortunately impossible.

At first, I was deeply disappointed. However, I went home and did a Google search. I found out about the Direct Commission Program the Army Reserve had put in place. I sent emails to a list of recruiters I found on the internet. Out of twelve emails sent, I received one reply. That email was from the South Carolina recruiter who helped me complete the process.

When I set a goal to come to America, my visa application was rejected three times. They said I wasn't qualified. However, from 2001 to 2004, not a single year passed that I didn't reapply. My original plan, which was to get my visa at the age of twenty-one years old and start my new life in America, went out the window pretty quickly. But after the setback, I modified my plan and kept going to the embassy until I was granted the visa.

My advice to you is to take time to know what you want to accomplish. Then devote the rest of your life and all your efforts to achieving that. Life is very serious business, and you only get to live it once. Stop trying to accomplish millions of things at the same time. Focus, and you will see results.

You will never have the energy to do everything you want in your life, but you will have enough to do the necessary things. Make your life count by setting goals that are important to you. As you achieve them one by one, you will soon realize that you are winning the game of life.

Imagination

The last thing I want to talk about in this chapter is your imagination. How are you using this powerful gift? Are you using it as your ally, or are you letting it ruin you? Robert Collier once said, "The great, successful men of the world have used their imagination! They think ahead and create their mental picture in all its details, filling in here, adding a little there, altering this a bit and that a bit, but steadily building, steadily building."

To create anything you want, you must first imagine it! Just think about your life today. Can you say that your present situation—or at least part of it—is the result of something you imagined? In case you haven't realized, your imagination is a sophisticated capability that you can use to bring anything you truly desire into your life. This is nothing mystical; it is part of you.

Everything we see today came from someone's imagination. Stop for a moment. Think about that.

The life you are trying so hard to achieve must first be conceived and nourished in your imagination. When I ask acquaintances what they desire out of life, I'm almost always surprised to hear that they just want to be rich and happy. We all desire to be rich and happy, but this desire is too vague. You must be able to vividly envision every aspect of the life you truly desire to live, from your environment to your relationships to your career. Conceive of them fully in your mind, and then imagine yourself living that life over and over again until you believe it.

Your imagination is the preview of the life you desire to live, so if your imagination is not clear enough about the specifics of that life, frustration and confusion are the guaranteed outcome.

I have achieved many victories through imagination long before the results I was seeking materialized. I cannot tell you how many times I've sat down for twenty or thirty minutes and just imagined the person I wanted to become, the kind of car I wanted to drive, the places I wanted to go, and things I wanted to do.

It is not enough to do this exercise one time and let it go. Get in the habit of doing this day after day until it becomes part of you. Use your thoughts to create your future. Allow yourself to dream. There is nothing to be afraid of. Let your mind go. Enjoy imagining.

You must change your mindset from I cannot to I can. How do you do that? You must read books, watch videos, and listen to motivational and inspirational speeches. If you don't have time, go on YouTube and just look up videos—there are thousands of them. In my personal experience, it takes an average of twenty-one days to create new habits. So, create new habits, and make them your master. Your habits will forge your new destiny. Everything is in your imagination, and it is up to you to think and believe. Then and only then will your desires materialize.

Lastly, your imagination must be consistent. To be effective, you must concentrate on one thing at the time. Focus. You cannot be effective in bringing something specific into your life if you are not focused. Therefore, take time to narrow down your major goal. Be relentless in pursuing it with your imagination.

This must become your only focus until you bring it into your reality. I am amazed how people will tell you about their most important goal or desire one day, and strive for something completely different the next.

Building a successful life is similar to building a house: it must be done brick by brick according to a very specific set of instructions. When I look back at my life, this principle has guided the majority of my accomplishments, and it is currently helping me build my future.

I will close this chapter with some of the quotes that inspired me to forge my destiny:

> *The reason most people never reach their goals is that they don't define them, or ever seriously consider them as believable or achievable. Winners can tell you where they are going, what they plan to do along the way, and who will be sharing the adventure with them.* —Denis Waitley

> *You have to set goals that are almost out of reach. If you set a goal that is attainable without much work or thought, you are stuck with something below your true talent and potential.* —Steve Garvey

> *By recording your dreams and goals on paper, you set in motion the process of becoming the person you most want to be. Put your future in good hands—your own.* —Mark Victor Hansen

I think imagination is at the heart of everything we do. Scientific discoveries couldn't have happened without imagination. Art, music, and literature couldn't exist without imagination. And so anything that strengthens imagination, and reading certainly does that, can help us for the rest of our lives. —Lloyd Alexander

We are what we pretend to be, so we must be careful about what we pretend to be. —Kurt Vonnegut

Imagination is everything. It is the preview of life's coming attractions. —Albert Einstein

I believe that the imagination is the passport we create to take us into the real world. I believe the imagination is another phrase for what is most uniquely us. —John Guare,

Imagination will often carry us to worlds that never were, but without it we go nowhere. —Carl Sagan

CHAPTER 8
Your Time

Time is the most valuable coin in your life. You and you alone will determine how that coin will be spent. Be careful that you do not let other people spend it for you. —Carl Sandburg

Bryant Tracy said, and I agree, "Time management is life management." Every day represents a micro portion of your entire life on earth. Whether you are rich or poor, everybody is given twenty-four hours per day and 365 days per year (except during leap years, when you get additional day).

How you use your time will determine where you will go in life. There are so many distractions in the world we live in. From TV to social media, never in the history of humankind have we been exposed to so much information every second of the day. With our smartphones and tablets we basically have the entire world of information, entertainment, and distraction at our fingertips, which makes it very hard to concentrate. We have become the subject of "mass thinking," and we rarely take time to engage with anything carefully. Instead, we spend hours scrolling and clicking on whatever catches our attention in the moment.

We are constantly bombarded with suggestions and notifications.

As we check our phones, tasks that could take us fifteen minutes stretch into two hours or more. We cannot focus for even five to ten minutes without interruption. This is taking away our precious time without us realizing it.

If you want to go somewhere with your life, you should focus and account for every hour of your day. You need to designate distraction-free time to concentrate on your major activities.

Your life will reflect the way you use your time. Your entire existence is composed of years, months, weeks, days, hours, minutes, and seconds, and the minutes, hours, days, weeks, months, and years you waste can never be recovered. So, every time you put off that education you know you need, every time you postpone going to the gym, and every time you procrastinate on anything you need to do to get that promotion, you are hurting yourself.

Sleep and work take up over half of every day. Depending on where you live and work, your commute could be short or long. You take time getting ready for work, eating, and doing many other things. Each of these peel away your time.

Then after work, the biggest time suck is the television. A recent study found that, in the average U.S. household, the television is on seven hours per day. That's like spending four months a year doing nothing but watching TV!

Couldn't you be using that time to do something productive? Every time you turn on your TV, ask yourself who you would rather be: the person on the other side of the screen, who is making money and enjoying his or her life, or the person wasting time watching through the screen?

I am not advocating getting rid of your TV altogether. But if you are like me, doing your best to get somewhere in life, you should use your time intelligently. If you are not where you want to be in your life, then you don't have any time to waste. Remember that there is not enough time to do everything you want, but there is enough time to do the most important things. Once you identify what you need to do, then you can no longer afford to be wasting time.

The second thing I want to talk about is procrastination. This is a disease, and it needs to be treated as such. The bottom line is that you must take control of your time. Do what you need to do now, and don't put off anything that needs to be done. You must develop a sense of urgency in order to make things happen. Once time is gone, you might never catch up.

Here are few tips on how to use your time better:

1. Write down everything on your to do list each day.

2. Ask yourself, "If I could only do three things today, what should they be?"

3. Focus on the list, and don't do anything that is not on it.

4. Prioritize all your activities.

5. Always ask yourself this question: "What is the best use of my time right now"?

6. Plan your relaxing time ahead, and make sure you set aside time to relax and do fun activities.

7. Use your personal calendar and always look ahead.

8. Be a time-conscious person.

9. Finally, once you have done what is important and necessary to move your life into the direction of your choosing, then you can binge watch your favorite shows and scroll your Facebook page.

10. Your time is your life, manage it well.

CHAPTER 9
Success: How Do You Define It?

Success means doing the best we can with what we have. Success is in the doing, not the getting; in the trying, not the triumph. Success is a personal standard, reaching for the highest that is in us, becoming all that we can be. —Zig Ziglar

I have come across many definitions of success. My favorite comes from an American icon on personal development, Earl Nightingale, who once said, "Success is the progressive realization of worthy goals." Take a few seconds to read this definition again.

I'm not sure how you define success or what being successful means to you, but this definition sums up my belief. For many, however, success equals money, fame, and nothing else. A narrow view of success often leads to a life of hopelessness and desolation.

Often, we are bombarded with the glamorous life on TV, movies, commercials, and other media that attempts to define success for us. It's easy to get lost in all the glitz and the glam.

I am the first to admit that I have fallen for this glamorous definition of success. I thought everything revolved around money and fame. But then I did more research on the topic. I realized that it's possible to be successful without having millions of dollars, being on TV, or being famous. The more I read the previous definition by Earl Nightingale, the more it made sense to me.

Life lived with a purpose is a successful life, so have a purpose for your life. If you are doing the things you set out to do, you are living a successful life. Time and time again, we all have looked at life through the lens of virtual reality and fantasies derived from TV and movies. Sometimes we are fooled into believing that until we own a BMW, a Mercedes-Benz, Bentley, and a Jaguar, we are not successful. We've bought into the idea that owning anything less than a twelve-bedroom house with a pool, basketball court, and movie theatre means we are not relevant.

But luxury yachts, flashy clothes, and jewelry do not define success. Luxury success ideas have done so much damage to our self-esteem that they've robbed us of the victories we achieved through our own hard work.

Being successful means setting goals and being disciplined enough to achieve them. When I discovered this fundamental truth, my focus shifted from acquiring money and fame to building the kind of life that has meaning to me.

I encourage you to examine your definition of success and adjust your thinking accordingly. This can relieve you of a great deal of pressure and set you on your way to happiness.

I will repeat it again: When you wake up every morning and do things that are important to your life, you are successful!

Now, as we've discussed, realizing important goals requires hard work and discipline. This is where people who are successful can be separated from people who are not. Successful people get in the habit of doing things a certain way that unsuccessful people do not. For example, everybody wants to have a great-paying job, but not everybody will be willing to get the required education or training for that job. Success is a do-it-yourself program, and it must come from you. You are the only one who knows what's most important to you.

It's also important to remember that success looks different to each of us, because we all have different life journeys. When I came to the United States, I could not formulate one single sentence in English. I didn't know much about American society and culture. So, at the age of twenty-four, when most Americans finish college and enter the workforce, I was watching children's programs to learn English. Back then success, for me, was all about ABC and 123.

Someone else might have looked at me and laughed. It was so elementary. But for me, these small goals were everything. They were the foundation that would allow me to achieve my bigger goals and dreams.

To the degree that we are able to do the things that are important to us, we are each successful in our own right. So, don't let anybody else define what you should or should not celebrate as a success. The road of your life journey won't always be an easy ride. You might have to stop sometimes, reevaluate, take a break, and detour before you arrive at your destination. But no matter what, it's your road, and you define success.

As you can see, my road from Togo to today wasn't a straight one. So, I encourage you to start congratulating yourself on all your achievements—big or small.

Besides you and a few other people who might read these lines, no one knows my name, and no paparazzi chases me down to take my pictures, but that doesn't limit or define my success. Success is personal, and I wish for you to find yours.

Before I leave the subject of success, let me remind you one more time that success is not a destination—it's a journey. Be true to yourself. Go after the life you know you desire, and celebrate your achievements. Your happiness depends on it.

CHAPTER 10
Problem Solving

A problem is a chance for you to use your immense potential, to do your best, to use your mind creatively." —Duke Ellington

I haven't met a single problem-free person in my life, and I don't believe you've met that person either. You will never be at a stage where you are totally free from life challenges unless you are eight feet under the ground in the cemetery.

Problems are here to stay, and being a functioning human being means figuring out the most effective ways to solve them. So whatever challenge you are facing, you are not the first, and you will not be the last.

In general, there are two kinds of problems you will face: the ones you cannot do anything about and the ones you definitely can. Learning to differentiate the two will greatly simplify your life. But for now, let's focus on the problems you can solve.

When faced with challenges, your best resource is your brain. When was the last time you effectively used it? It's so easy to turn to others for solutions, but more often than not, the people we turn to don't know any better than we do. I encourage you to research for yourself how you can solve your challenges.

First, you must identify the exact challenge you're facing. Many times, we don't know what to do because we haven't even clearly spelled out what it is that we are facing. In medicine, they say, "proper diagnosis is half the cure," and this is true for every challenge or issue in your life. If you can clearly articulate your challenge, I can guarantee you will find a solution.

Then, gather all the information pertaining to your situation. Ask questions, do research, think, compare, and analyze the whole situation—not just one single aspect—and then make a decision. Even if it is a wrong decision, it is better than no decision at all. For every challenge there is a solution, and it is your task to find it.

When it comes to solving most of your challenges, do not waste your time talking about them to people who cannot help you solve them. Remember, 90 percent don't care, 5 percent will pay you lip services, and even though the other 5 percent might want to help you, their priority will be their own problems. Instead, seek advice from experts in the area where you're struggling.

Here are some of the techniques I have used to solve most of my challenges:

1. Accept responsibility for every situation you find yourself in. Blaming someone is counterproductive and will not unleash your creativity.

2. Stop calling your challenges problems. When your mind is programmed to solve challenges, your creativity shuts down at the sound of the word "problem."

3. When your health is the issue, talk to your doctor or someone in the medical field. What good will it do to tell someone who doesn't know much as you do about medical conditions? All they can do is to speculate, and this will not cure you.

4. If money is the challenge, sit down with someone who has achieved some level of financial success.

5. Don't talk to your single friends about relationships issues. Look at the relationship status of the person giving you advice to determine whether they are qualified. You can also talk to your pastor, religious and spiritual leaders, or other qualified professionals to walk you through relationship challenges.

6. For how to conceive and achieve your goals, look to someone who has done it well. Ask questions.

7. Choose your mate or life partner wisely. What you see is what you get. People can change their own actions and their own plans. But you can't. You will exhaust yourself if you think you can change someone. You are only delaying your frustration and resentment if you settle for someone you don't really want. We all have made the mistake of thinking we could change someone. If you don't like a personality trait in a man or woman, and this is a deal breaker for you, make it known clearly and make your decision sooner instead of secretly hoping it will go away.

8. For every challenging situation, there is a solution. The bottom line here is that you need to get support from a credible source and credible person when facing adversities.

9. Remember that your friends and family might not be the right people to seek for advice. It's not that they don't love you or they don't care about you, but they simply might not know what you need to hear to help you with your situation.

Unfortunately, the first thing we all do when we run into a stumbling block is to call our friends, brothers, sisters, or whomever we are close to for advice. When we take action based on well-meaning but uneducated advice, we run the risk of worsening our situations.

You wouldn't ask a medical doctor to fix your car or your hairdresser to fix your computer, so don't seek advice for personal problems from someone who doesn't know what he or she is talking about. You have a great mind, so use it. Direct yourself appropriately.

Your challenges are opportunities to learn, grow, and move forward in your life. Become the person who looks at your challenges with an open mind, and watch your creativity set you free.

CHAPTER 11
Finances

The thing I have discovered about working with personal finance is that the good news is that it is not rocket science. Personal finance is about 80 percent behavior. It is only about 20 percent head knowledge.
—Dave Ramsey

Money, since its introduction into our society, has been a source of all kinds of problems to humans. Money doesn't solve all our problems, but I believe it can vastly contribute to happiness. I grew up without having much, and today I truly appreciate hard earned money and the comfort it brings. Having what we need can provide us with decent living conditions and better schools for our children. It can enable us to pay hospital bills, go on vacations, and live a comfortable life.

The major issue you and I have with money is that, in America, credit tempts us to spend far more than we earn. This habit can quickly jeopardize our financial health and put us in a hole. We get into the habit of thinking, "I will pay later", and gradually we find ourselves "robbing Peter to pay Paul."

Second, we tend to blindly seek more, never taking the time to figure out how much we really need to earn to sustain our current and future lifestyle.

Will Smith said, "We spend money that we do not have on things we do not need to impress people who do not care." Don't try to keep up with people on your left or right because you are trying to impress them. Spend and save wisely, according to your own needs.

We tend to think that, if we only had a million dollars, all our financial issues would be resolved. This is not true. Millionaires have money problems, too. The more you earn, the more you spend. The key is to earn more than you spend and keep a good control on your financial behavior.

I have picked up some good financial advice along my journey, and I would like to share it with you. My formula for financial independence, which increased my happiness, is to spend less than I earn. Then save. And then invest.

You need a plan that will serve as a roadmap to your financial destination. I have created a financial plan based on my income and expenses, and I watch carefully how I spend money. Take inventory of finances; and be honest. If you are deep in debt, find a way to stop debt growth. Analyze your spending habits, and I guarantee you will find where to start adjusting.

The first good habit to develop is saving. Always save 10 percent of your income. Put it in a separate account—one you won't touch—before paying your rent, mortgage, loans, or anything else. If you cannot save 10 percent, then start with what you can, and increase it gradually.

If you don't have a rich family member who left you an inheritance, then you belong to the majority of us who need to work hard and smart to become financially independent. There is no other practical way. Forget about get-rich-quick schemes—they are nothing but illusions.

Second, determine how much you really need to sustain your monthly expenses for decent living conditions. For some, it might be $2,000; for others, it might be $5,000 or more. The key here is to determine what you need to earn.

Third, have a budget every month. Write down your income and expenses on paper to see how you are spending your money.

Fourth, allocate every dollar you earn on paper first before any spending. I have heard so many people say, "I don't know where all my money went!" This blindness is a bad habit. You must know where every dollar goes.

Fifth, delay every big purchase and ask yourself, "Do I need this, or do I want this?" There is a huge difference between need and want. We want many things that we don't really need.

Once you've learned to control your spending, save money every month, and invest wisely. Watch what happens to you financially in the next three, five, and ten years. Don't buy a very expensive car just because you want to impress somebody—you will be the one stuck with the car payments for years. Don't be impulsive with your money. Instead, always ask yourself why you need to spend that money.

Managing your money habits will greatly affect how you feel about yourself. Very few people are really educated on financial decision-making and on things like credit cards, college debts, cars loans, and home mortgages. Money management is a very important and serious topic. I encourage you to stay vigilant. Get educated, read, and study this subject.

Finally, I highly recommend Napoleon Hill's book, Think and Grow Rich! Even the title is pertinent, as our lives are mostly affected by the way we think. Poor thinking habits keep most people poor. Most people work hard, but they don't think big. Your mind builds upon the way you think, so think big, and act smart. The fundamental rules to becoming financially free are to spend less than you earn, save at least 10 percent of your income every time, and do not spend money you haven't earned.

CHAPTER 12
I am an American Soldier

In John F. Kennedy's inaugural address on January 20, 1961, the newly elected president famously told the country, "My fellow Americans: Ask not what your country can do for you; ask what you can do for your country."

This chapter is dedicated to all my brothers and sisters in arms—past, present, and future!

October 1, 2010, is a date I will never forget. It is on this day that I said "I do" to the American people. I raised my right hand and swore to "Defend and protect the Constitution of the United States of America against all enemies foreign and domestic." Little did I know that this solemn ceremony in the Military Entry Processing Center of Charlotte, North Carolina, would open doors to a life of service and opportunities I never knew existed.

As a first-generation immigrant from Togo, I was often asked what an immigrant like myself was doing in the United States Army. My reply to this question was always, "Why not?" Then I'd pause and elaborate a little more.

When I left my country of origin back in 2004, I never thought that I would one day serve in a foreign military. Between 2004 and

2010, I spent six years working and searching in my new country. I didn't finish college like I wanted, I was working unsatisfying jobs, I barely had any money after paying all my bills, and I was pretty much stuck in the same place.

Nothing was going like I wanted. I saw my dreams dissolve one by one. I didn't have anyone to rely on, and I always felt that there was more to my life that the situation I was in.

In the summer of 2010, when I was driving a taxicab in Louisville, Kentucky, working thirteen our days, six or seven days a week, a customer on his way to the airport gave me the advice that would change my life.

As a cab driver, I enjoyed engaging my clients in conversation, though most of it was limited to weather, sports, news, and other small talk. The gentleman I picked up that morning was very friendly and asked me general questions about where I was from and my goals in life. As I told him a little about myself and what I was trying to do, he quickly advised me to me to check out the U.S. Army. His exact words were, "Dude, you can get your citizenship and go to college for free." Just as he finished that sentence, we arrived at the departure terminal. He was in a hurry to catch his flight, so he wished me good luck with everything and left.

I don't even remember his name, and I wouldn't recognize him if I saw him again, but I will never forget the advice he threw at me on the fly. This total stranger was so right. The U.S. Army became the family that I didn't have in the United States.

Through my life of service, this great country has given me a blank check to write my own ticket in life. I truly believe that if a new immigrant or any young man or woman wants to get a head start in life or learn about this country and its culture, a few years in the military is a great way to do it.

In my short army career, I had the privilege to meet people from every corner of this nation. I traveled to many different states and countries for training exercises and deployments. I met some of the most incredible leaders who do their jobs quietly with pride and passion.

I believe a lot of people love the idea of being in the military, but in reality, very few actually do it. In fact, less than one percent of the American population serves in the armed forces.

Before joining the army, I had never seen young people believe so much in their country. Being in the U.S. Army opened my eyes to a particular group of people who are ready and willing to give up everything, including their lives, to defend this nation. They aren't on the clock Monday to Friday, nine to five. They know they will miss birthdays, they know they will not be there when their children take their first steps, and they know no holidays are guaranteed.

Despite these sacrifices, they take so much pride in serving. When I ask my fellow soldiers why they joined this unique brotherhood, I am always humbled by the incredible responses. Among many, the love of the country is always one of the top reasons.

I joined the Army Reserve as an enlisted soldier, with the rank of private and no college degree, in October, 2010. After completing my basic training and advanced individual training at Fort Leonard Wood in Missouri, I came back to my first unit in Salisbury, North Carolina.

Nine months later I requested a transfer to a much closer unit in Greensboro, North Carolina: 422nd Civil Affairs Battalion, also knowns as the "Centurions." It was in this unit that my army career really took off. Many soldiers, officers, and enlisted alike impacted greatly my career. These are just a few.

Brigadier General (currently) Robert Cooley was the battalion commander of 422 Civil Affairs Unit, and he never stopped telling me how much potential I had. He gave me the opportunity to brief the entire battalion leadership every month and advised me to become an officer.

During our monthly training, as an enlisted soldier with the rank of specialist, I was hesitant to brief the entire command. I was insecure about my accent, my rank, and how new I was to the army. However, the opportunity then-Lieutenant Colonel Cooley gave me forced me to learn quickly, and it built my confidence. I am forever grateful to General Cooley for believing in me.

Sergeant First Class (Retired) Duane Robinson: To this day, I have never met a non-commissioned officer as devoted as Sergeant First Class Robinson. The first time I met Sergeant Robinson was during our monthly battle assembly in early 2012. As the other soldiers and I stood around in the drill hall, I saw Sergeant Robinson walking around the room with a sheet of paper in his hand, asking soldiers about when they could attend army schools and other trainings.

There is a saying in the Army Reserve: "You are in charge of your own career." All this means is that you are responsible for how and where your career progresses. From my experience, it was rare to see a senior non-commissioned officer asking soldiers about what school they wanted to go to and when they could go.

Sergeant Robinson went above and beyond to mentor and help younger soldiers further their careers. I was one these soldiers.

Major Perkins and Ms. Davis: There was no time during my time with this unit or after I left that I needed a document signed—or had any other request—that Ms. Davis or Major Perkins could not help me out. Beyond developing great working relationships, I became friends with both over the years. In fact, to this day, I can always call them for any reason or no reason at all.

When I needed letters of recommendation during the process of becoming an officer, Lieutenant-Colonel Cooley, Major Perkins and SFC Robinson (Ret) wrote flattering observations about me and my potential. Their endorsements ultimately allowed me to become army officer, and I can't begin to describe the impact they had on my life.

Basic Officer Leadership Course in Fort Lee, Virginia

During my Basic Officer Leadership Course at Fort Lee, Virginia, I met many more leaders who were going to all four corners of the world to serve our Nation. Among them, I would like to introduce you to two officers in my class: Second Lieutenant Spencer Bentley and Second Lieutenant Jimmy Cardona, who embody just how incredible and diverse our great army is.

Lieutenant Spencer Bentley was twenty-two years old, freshly out of college and heading to Hawaii for his first duty station after graduation.

Lieutenant Jimmy Cardona was forty-two years old, and he had served twenty-plus years in the United States Air Force active duty, before joining the Army Reserve. I asked both officers about their backgrounds and their decisions to join the army and serve as officers.

Here is Lieutenant Bentley in his own words:

"I am from a suburb of Columbus, Ohio, called Pickerington. I lived in Pickerington with my older brother, older sister, mom, and dad. My mom always said that, since I was a little kid, she knew I would want to join the military.

"After playing soccer and running track in high school, I enlisted in the Ohio National Guard. I joined the ROTC (Reserve Officer Training Corps) program at Ohio University shortly after. I attended Ohio University, studying entrepreneurship for all four years, and I loved it. I felt like I was becoming a well-rounded and diverse individual as I discovered the world of business and developed my leadership through the ROTC Program.

"When I am asked why I decided to pledge my life to defend and protect this great country, it is almost difficult to answer. I have always had this feeling that I wanted to do more for those around me, and I wanted to serve this country. For me this led to learning about the military and later deciding on the army as my branch of choice. I want to be the one that does the job that others do not want to do, to take the unwanted job so others do not have to do it. Not only do I get the pleasure of serving the country, but I get to see different parts of the nation and the world. I get to talk to people from all different cultures, hear their stories, and learn from them. This is an amazing world, and I would not change my decision to join the army for anything."

Second Lieutenant Bentley was accepted to Army Rangers School before even graduating from Basic Officer Leadership Course. I truly admired this young man, who is full of ambition and potential.

When I asked Second Lieutenant Cardona why he joined the army at his age after serving a little over two decades in the air force, he simply replied, "I still have something to offer my country." Lieutenant Cardona was born in Colombia, South America, and he came to United States when he was two years old. He joined the air force right out of high school and never looked back.

As I listened to their stories, I thought to myself, "This is what makes this nation so unique." This country has a place for everybody as long as you are willing to pay the price for what you want. After twenty-plus years of service in one branch, Second Lieutenant Cardona was still willing to commit more years to another branch, and a young man in his early twenties decided to dedicate all he had to the life of service. To all my classmates:

LT Albanese Anthony

LT Bentley Spencer

LT Bray Isaac

LT Camp Jonathan

LT Cardona Jimmy

LT Carey Gerald

LT Carroll Adam

LT Dancy Eric

LT Darby Adrianne

Dees William (Department of Army Civilian)

LT Denzil Dennison

LT Dominguez Abraham

LT Dorsey Margaret

LT Gale James

LT Gallwoay Kevin

LT Gillespey Tyler

LT Hagen Jon

LT Hoffman Evan

LT Hollier Adam

LT Hoxha Klita

LT Huynh Thomas

LT Jones Nathan

Langlois Joshua (Department of Army Civilian)

LT Lor Sengxai

LT Lown Wesley

LT Lynn Mark

LT Murphy Jamal

LT Ostheim Jonathan

LT Pinchuk Igor

LT Porterfield Keely

LT Pugh Samuel

LT Quinn Brian

LT San Nicolas Javelin

LT Sezgin Onur

LT Smith DeAnthony

LT Storto Alex

LT Vinluan Mark

LT Wells Joshua

LT Wentling Jonathan

Thank you for your service and your dedication to our Nation. It was a pleasure studying, sharing and working together through our Basic Officer Leadership Course at Fort Lee, Virginia. To our instructor CPT Forrister, thank you for your mentorship.

The U.S. Army provided me the opportunity to go to college for free and helped me become a United States citizen much more quickly than I could have on my own. The army gave me healthcare coverage, a guaranteed home loan, and so many more benefits. But those tangible gifts are just a small part of what the military has given me. I cannot measure the value of serving in the finest military this world has seen, with the finest people I've ever met. The bonds my fellow service members and I formed will last a lifetime.

I am certainly aware that not everybody can or will serve in the military; however, I urge all new immigrants and all young men and women who meet the requirements to serve this great country: do it! I can promise that your life will never be the same.

Even if the military is not your path, I challenge you to get involved in something greater than yourself. Whichever way you can, embark on a life of service to your family, your community, and your country.

I will close this chapter by sharing the Soldier's Creed. These lines have had a powerful impact on me, and I want you to have the opportunity to reflect on this unique philosophy:

The Soldier's Creed

I am an American soldier.

I am a warrior and a member of a team.

I serve the people of the United States and live the Army values.

I will always place the mission first.

I will never accept defeat.

I will never quit.

I will never leave a fallen comrade.

I am disciplined, physically and mentally tough, trained, and proficient in my warrior tasks and drills.

I always maintain my arms, my equipment, and myself.

I am an expert, and I am a professional.

I stand ready to deploy, engage, and destroy the enemies of the United States of America in close combat.

I am a guardian of freedom and the American way of life.

I am an American Soldier.

These words are forever engraved in my heart and I consider service to my country as the biggest honor and privilege I've been granted. I am proud to wear the uniform of the United States Army, and I am endlessly grateful to the American people for this honor.

About Faith

I haven't talked much about the role of faith, and I won't dwell on it here because I believe that faith is highly personal. Religion is just one of many ways individuals can choose to exercise their faith—

whatever that looks like to them.

But I can't leave you without telling you how important my faith has been in my life. It kept me from going overboard whenever the going got tough. I don't know where or who I would be today without my deep belief that God is out there somewhere, working on my behalf. This perspective has allowed me to be patient and resilient when nothing seemed to be working in my favor.

I am not here to advocate any particular faith or spiritual life, but I do believe it is very important to nurture this aspect of your life, whether you believe in God, the universe, or some other entity. Please find time to connect with your God and to be in touch with your spiritual side. Spiritual time will generate a new energy in your life every time you run into a wall. And there will be many walls between you and your major life goals. Believe me.

Your deep convictions, your perseverance, and your drive to make something out of yourself and help others will lift you up, with the help of your spiritual energy. Persistence is simply a demonstration of your faith in yourself. I encourage you to not ignore this.

On Courage

Many of us think courage is the absence of fear. However, I believe that being courageous means acting despite your fears. You will be better off acknowledging that life is a challenge. The psychological pressure we face every day can break us down if we do not have the courage to fight to change our conditions. Even if you are born into material riches, you still need to have a psychologically balanced life to function.

The way you exercise your courage will determine the outcome of your toughest situations. It takes courage to keep going to work after you have been passed up for promotion. It takes courage to be honest with yourself and admit your faults. It takes courage to keep trying after experiencing defeat.

I promised myself that, no matter where my life went, I would never stop trying. I might take a break, I might cry, and I might be sad, mad, or upset for days, but I would go back and keep trying until I could make the changes I wanted to make. Since the day I made this promise to myself, I have been able to put all my worries away and live at peace with myself.

The truth is that we are all afraid of something. The big challenge is to act despite your fears. When faced with a challenge, don't let your fears control you. Be courageous and then act. Your fears will disappear, and your confidence level will increase.

On Forgiveness

Holding a grudge against someone makes you that person's prisoner, so free yourself of grudges. When you harbor anger, the person you're angry with controls your mood and your emotions and keeps you off balance. Why would you give anyone so much power?

Forgiveness is for you, not for the other person. Many times, we think that forgiving somebody makes us weak, but the opposite is true. It takes a strong person to apologize for a wrongdoing. It requires just as much strength to forgive.

So, when you've done wrong, apologize. It doesn't mean that you are weak; it means that you know yourself well enough—and value others enough--to admit you've done something wrong.

And when people have done you wrong, forgive them, and free yourself from that negativity.

Above all forgive yourself every day for all the unwise things you have done and the mistakes you have made. We are our own worst critics, but it doesn't have to be that way.

FINAL THOUGHTS ABOUT YOUR JOURNEY

*The most difficult work you will ever do is the work on yourself.
Learn to work harder on yourself than you do in your job. If you
work harder on job you will make a living, but if you work harder
on yourself you will make a fortune.* —Jim Rohn

Lastly, every life on this earth is a journey. From the time you were born to the time you die; many things will happen to you. Some will be within your control, but many will not. For example, we don't decide when or where we are born, how we grow up, or who our parents are. But as human beings, we have the remarkable ability to change who we are and where we are heading. Establish the awareness to build our own roadmaps and the drive to follow them.

Those four-dollar Tracy Brian tapes revolutionized my entire life, and they're just the tip of the iceberg. The United States of America is the country it is because of all the formidable people and ideas here. There is a saying that knowledge is power, and to that I would add: applied knowledge is an unstoppable force.

Whether you accept them or not, our universe has principles that govern our existence on earth. You cannot choose how your life begins, but you can change its course once you learn and apply those principles. You can either blame your life circumstances or work with what you have in order to forge your destiny—the choice is yours.

I am not sure where this book finds you. I don't know your current circumstances, your life story, or your season of life, but I know there is something utterly unique about you.

Winning the game of life is not about having millions of dollars in bank, having the most expensive things, or living like a Hollywood star. It is about taking the necessary steps toward the small things that really matter to you.

Bigger struggles will make it harder to achieve your victories—not impossible. For some, graduating from high school or college, buying a house for the first time, commissioning as an officer in the United States Army, or getting a stable job in the career field of their choosing will be an easy victory. However, for those like me and you, who started from nothing and clawed our way up, achieving those goals is heaven on earth—those victories are everything we could possibly wish for.

So, someone who's never walked in your shoes might perceive your victories as irrelevant or small. My advice to you is to avoid those types of people.

Instead, celebrate your achievements—even the smallest ones— any way you can. These celebrations will galvanize your spirit, mind, and body, and they'll encourage you to go after more and bigger goals.

Coming to the United States with nothing, learning English, joining the army, earning U.S. Citizenship, graduating from college, becoming an Army Officer, achieving a six-figure income, becoming a valuable member of my family, community, and country, owning houses and cars, and building a strong personal and financial foundation in fourteen years may seem like a miracle—or at the very least, great luck.

However, there is nothing mysterious, lucky, or miraculous about my journey. I have worked on myself, and I am continuously working on becoming better. You can also become better no matter where you are in your life. Decide today. Everything I achieved came through hard work, struggles, perseverance, and the undying belief that I would make something out of myself or die trying.

I made up my mind very early that would live my one life fully. I accepted early that pains and failures would be part of life, but so would joy, triumphs, and achievements. I accepted that I would never be perfect or good at everything, but that I could do something to improve myself every day in a specific area.

My biggest accomplishment is the person I became along my journey. I learned a lot and continue to do so. I became more patient and tolerant, and I learned to see life with open heart in my fourteen years living in America.

The United States of America is known around the world as the beacon of freedom, the Land of Liberty, the refuge for the oppressed, and the place of new beginnings. Personally, the United States is where I discovered myself and created an amazing life.

I made the most vital discovery I ever made—the power of thinking my way into anything I set my mind to—here in America. But the principles I spoke about in this book are universal. My intention now is to help others learn this way of living and benefit from applying these principles to their lives.

No matter where you are currently—physically, spiritually, emotionally, or financially—you can transform your life by beginning to think and work your way into good health, prosperity, peace of mind, success, and happiness. The choice is yours.

I wish you happiness, I wish you love, and above all I wish you to discover the true purpose of your life and dance to your own music. I encourage you to get busy.

Love,

Komi M. Afetse

A THANK YOU

As willful and determined I am to achieve my dreams, I couldn't have done all this without the support and assistance of my family (immediate and extended), friends and many other people who knowingly or unknowingly aided me along my journey. My children particularly became my motivation to leave behind a legacy they will be proud of.

So, I wake up every day knowing that there are people who believe in me and I must do everything in my power not to let them down. I fight for a better future that will benefit all of us.

I take this opportunity to recognize every kind and not-so-kind soul I encountered these last fourteen years. All contributed to me becoming the person I am today.

About the Author

Born in Togo, a country in West Africa, Komi Afetse left his homeland in search of a better life in the United States of America in March, 2004. After a very difficult start in the United States, he joined the army and became a naturalized U.S. citizen in August, 2011. He later graduated from North Carolina A&T State University in Greensboro with a bachelor's degree in international relations.

As a civil affairs and psychological operation non-commissioned officer, he was deployed in Djibouti (Horn of Africa) between 2014 and 2015 in support of a U.S. Government mission in that region. He later earned his commission as an officer in the U.S. Army Reserve. He is currently a serving as U.S. Army Reserve Officer and works as an information technology professional for the U.S. Department of Defense in Washington, D.C.

Komi Afetse's remarkable life story is part of a bigger story that is "The American Dream." This is the story of hard work, perseverance, resilience, faith, and determination. Komi joined the army at the lowest enlisted rank, with no college degree, and quickly rose to become an officer.

When he came to the United States, Komi could not even spell his own name in English, and his journey to personal success and financial independence is a testimony to his determination, his daring, and his trust in this incredible country's principles and opportunities.

Author of many essays on self-development, self-motivation, goal-setting, and inspirational living, Komi is a motivational speaker and a founder of human development consulting company Afetse Consulting International. He is a world traveler and public advocate for successful living.

For more information about the author, speaking engagements, and bulk book orders, please visit: https://komiafetse.com/

Made in the USA
Middletown, DE
19 February 2022